Personal Reputation Management

Making the internet work for you

Louis Halpern & Roy Murphy

Halpern Cowan
172A Arlington Road
London
NW1 7HL
Tel: +44 20 7284 9700
www.halperncowan.com

ISBN 978-0-9562892-0-9

Design and text by Halpern Cowan

Every possible effort has been made to ensure that the information contained in this book is accurate at the time of going to press, and the publisher and authors cannot accept any responsibility for any errors or omissions, however caused. Publisher and authors accept no responsibility for any loss or damage occasioned to any person acting or refraining from acting as a result of the material contained in this book.

This book is sold with the understanding that neither the publisher nor authors are engaged in rendering legal or other professional services. If legal or other expert assistance is required, the services of a competent professional should be sought.

All references to companies, company logos and company products or services, including case studies, are for information purposes only. References to companies do not constitute an endorsement of such company or its products or services.

All references to individuals, including case studies, are for informational purposes only. Such references are based upon review of google search results of the individual and neither the publisher nor authors endorse the content of any such google search result.

About the Authors

Louis Halpern

With more than 17 years' experience in technology, marketing and business development, Louis has assisted the growth of blue chip companies, SMEs and numerous executives.

Louis is the CEO of a rapidly growing innovative top 30 UK digital agency, Halpern Cowan, where he has personally recruited a number of clients ranging from Aviva to Malmaison, Herbalife and Supernanny.

Prior to founding Halpern Cowan, Louis worked at the highest level with firms such as UBS, HSBC, Financial Software, Lycos, Schroders, and United Business Media.

With contributions to *New Media Age* and *The Guardian* newspaper, he is a highly regarded authority on his fields of expertise including Website Design & Build, Search Engine Marketing and connecting people and brands with Social Media. His blog, Louis Halpern's View, is widely read.

Twitter: **twitter.com/louis999**
Blog: **www.louishalpern.com**

Roy Murphy

Roy Murphy is a creative director, writer, and branding expert. He has worked at several well respected advertising agencies and with clients including Motorola, Disney, Virgin, Harrods, Paul Smith, Herbalife and Aviva.

A first class BSc graduate in *media technology*, he has been advising individuals and businesses on how to use creativity to maximise their visibility for over 12 years.

He still loves to create and deliver knockout ideas that gain maximum attention, from viral marketing to traditional advertising campaigns. He currently lectures undergraduates at Greenwich University on topics inlcuding personal branding and real world creativity.

Twitter: **twitter.com/roymurphy**

Contents

Overview 9

1   Introduction 15

2   The history of reputation management 39

3   Everyone's famous now 55

4   The law and your reputation 67

5   Social media 77

6   Defining yourself online 85

7   Tools & technology 111

8   Getting people, search engines and social   153
     networks to notice you

9   Maintaining your personal reputation   181

     References   201

     Image Credits   205

     Glossary   211

     Notes   221

Overview of reputation management and what's inside this book

"It takes many good deeds to build a good reputation, and only one bad one to lose it"

Benjamin Franklin

Who is this book for?

Anyone who values their reputation, and who understands that promoting and protecting it is now a major factor in achieving their professional objectives.

Simply put, your reputation affects you. It affects your ability to get a new job, to keep your existing one, to help or hinder customers purchasing from your company or brand, and your chances of gaining a competitive business advantage.

Ask yourself this question: what is my reputation worth and can I afford to leave it to chance?

Why is reputation so important?

With global financial systems in meltdown and uncertainty in the job and housing market, one of the best investments you can make is in the ownership and control of your own reputation. The importance of promoting yourself as an individual or as part of your company is becoming more prevalent, and is often the difference between success and failure in today's job and business market. The internet is where the battle for your reputation is taking place. So why not use the internet to your advantage?

Don't let someone else own your reputation

- Turn on your computer, open up your favourite internet browser and type in your own name. What did you find?

- Did you find various other people with the same name as you? Would you want an employer, recruiter or customer to think they were you?

- Did you find nothing about yourself? If you can't find anything, neither will your next employer or business contact.

- Did you find that your name was mentioned several times but that each results was related to outdated content or jobs? If so, you are in danger of falling behind in today's combative economic environment.

- Did you find that search results were returned under your name but they were not how you would like to be presented? Perhaps you found a link to a social media website such as Facebook, Flickr or MySpace, with pictures of you larking about on holiday or on a stag weekend?

- Did you find defamatory content about you or your company? Malicious competitors, disgruntled colleagues or even ex-friends can quickly and easily affect your reputation.

If you see yourself in any of these examples, you already understand the power of your reputation and the power of the internet in promoting and enhancing it. The reality is that today you must be consistently managing and monitoring your online reputation to ensure your professional profile remains a benefit to you.

Welcome to the brave new world of Personal Reputation Management. The stakes are high, so it's time to get to work.

What this book will do for you

This book will explain the value of promoting and protecting your reputation. It is a tough, competitive world out there and you need to be in control of your reputation – if you aren't, someone else will do so for you – and who's to know whether they'll be promoting or hindering your future prospects? No matter whether you are

- A new graduate trying to get your first foothold in the world of work;

- A second jobber keen to progress through the ranks of your organisation;

- Someone without a current job and in need of a competitive advantage to find another; or

- A business owner, manager or executive who wants to gain an edge over his or her competitors.

This book is relevant to you.

How do I best use this book?

This book is laid out in an easy to read way, so that you can pick up and run with any chapter while understanding how you can manage and promote your reputation quickly and efficiently. Throughout the book there are reputation actions. These can either be completed as you read through the book or together in one session – whatever your preference. We have also included a variety of tips and techniques, real-world case studies and other pointers throughout to help you gain a better understanding of the context of personal reputation management. We recommend reading the book sequentially, but you will get just as much out of it by dipping in and out of the chapters that you are most interested in.

This book is divided into two sections:

The first section puts your reputation into historical context, explains the hows and whys of reputation management, and demonstrates how it relates to your personal situation. Your personal brand and how you develop your own personal framework from which to promote a consistent, core message are covered in detail.

The second part of the book takes the shape of a practical guide to promoting and protecting your reputation using the internet. Learn how to find your audience and connect with employers, recruiters, businesses and customers alike. Find out how to use social networks and which social media tools and techniques can quickly improve your reputation. Discover how to monitor and manage your growing reputation so your target audience can find what you have to offer and you can learn new ways of promoting your key business asset: You.

Introduction to the chapters

▶ **Chapter 1: Introduction** – An overview of reputation management and why it matters to you. Being in control means not leaving your reputation to chance; you can do something about your reputation now: you can begin to manage it for the first time. Reputation actions challenge you to think about your current status online.

▶ **Chapter 2: A brief history of reputation** - Cavemen, kings, queens and paupers have understood for thousands of years that reputation can make you rich or cost your life. Social identity is still a fundamental aspect of the human state. Back to today, the growth of the internet means your character is history, your reputation is the most potent currency you have.

▶ **Chapter 3: Everyone's famous now** – You are never switched off; celebrity culture has come to your door and you are now public property. In a 24/7 world, you must find the right tactics to understand and control your reputation. Don't let the tail wag the dog, you are your own medium and message.

▶ **Chapter 4: The law and your reputation** – The internet is your reputation battleground and the rules of engagement have changed. Recourse to existing legal remedies may not be enough. You need to know the rules of the game and execute your plans with clinical efficiency. Libel and slander can be fought proactively online.

▶ **Chapter 5: Social media** – A wide connection of blogs, websites and networks are available for you to connect with your audience. Your audience is already talking about you on these networks. You must interact and influence these conversations in the right way to help build your reputation online.

▶ **Chapter 6: Defining yourself online** – This practical chapter helps you begin to define your reputation strategy and understand your key objectives in doing so. Through development of your online framework, you will create four strong pillars from which to build out your professional profile online. You are now a brand that needs to be promoted: your achievements, status, background and objectives are the key to achieving your professional aims.

▶ **Chapter 7: Tools and technology** – Understand the techniques you need to start promoting your reputation. Discover simple and effective strategies to develop websites, blogs and social media spaces. Find out which social media networks are right for you, how to set up your own webspace with advice on domain names, and how to write content that will get you noticed.

▶ **Chapter 8: Getting people, search engines and social networks to notice you** – Your audience must be able to find you; employers, recruiters, customers and search engines are looking for what you have to offer. Try out practical tactics to promote you across your online spaces to ensure that your message of quality, consistency and visibility is repeated again and again.

▶ **Chapter 9: Maintaining your personal reputation** – You have set up your professional profile and most of the hard work is done. Now you need to track what is being said about you online and know how to maximise your opportunities and react to any negative content. Learn the tweaks, tips and tricks that help you stay in control of your personal reputation online.

Remember: your reputation is your key professional asset

1

Introduction

Welcome to the beginning of your reputation management masterclass. Your reputation strategy starts here.

One of the City of London's foremost headhunters, Charles Young, viewed the financial crisis as an opportunity for his firm. But soon after giving his card out to dozens of recently redundant investment bank Lehman's staff, he started to receive calls alerting him to his online alter ego: Charles Young, adult entertainer. Potential candidates had 'Googled' him only to see his name superseded by one of the world's most well-known adult film stars. Not surprisingly, work was anything but brisk.

When TalkSPORT radio DJ Rod Lucas turned up for work in late November 2008, he was summarily dismissed. Why? His name appeared on a website as part of a leaked membership list for one of Britain's most controversial right-wing political parties. His pleas that his membership was 'for research purposes only' fell on deaf ears.

In January 2009, a photograph of superstar swimmer Michael Phelps was circulated in the British media. An image of him smoking what appeared to be an illegal substance was quickly copied and shared online. Overnight his hard-earned multi-million dollar sponsorship deals started to look rather less secure. Searching under 'Michael Phelps' on Google didn't just bring up his undoubtedly outstanding achievements in the swimming pool; what also came up were some rather less savoury links to the news allegations, affecting the positive reputation he worked years to achieve.

Google™

You

Google Search   **I'm Feeling Lucky**

But what has this got to do with me, you might ask?

The answer: everything.

Why personal reputation management matters to you

We have now reached a time where your personal reputation is available to be viewed by anyone, any time.

REPUTATION ACTION

✔ As an experiment, log on to your computer and type in your name on any search engine. The odds are that you will appear on one or more websites, not just in a professional capacity but also in a private, social capacity.

Even if you don't appear on a search listing, perhaps someone has the same name as you and appears in your place. Whatever the circumstances, if you don't appear on any search engine ranking then you can be assured you will do soon. Internet usage and the explosion in digital interaction through social media networks, blogs, *user generated sites (See user generated content)* and new technologies, has combined with your personal data footprint. It is expanding exponentially, and it's only a matter of time before you will appear on the internet in some way, shape or form.

In the internet age, your personal *'brand'* or identity is never off duty and your reputation is always 'switched on'.

The key question, therefore, is this: are you in control of what personal information appears on the internet about you?

No? Then you need to read on.

Bob James Did you hear about John, got fired today. I can't believe it. Do you know what happened?
2 hours ago · Comment · Like

 Chris Bennet Something about the office party but I'm not sure. He was pretty out of it that night. Who knows what he got up to?
📠 1 hour ago · Comment · Like

 Bob James I heard it was something to do with that bottle of tequila that was floating around!
10 mins ago · Comment · Like

1.2 Who is listening to your online conversations?

The end of privacy

Privacy is in the past. It's gone. It's history.

The UK Government has adopted legislation whereby every email and web search that you perform is recorded and logged into a vast computer bank. When you're searching on the internet, the UK Government knows what you do, when you do it and keeps a record to prove it. The same country leads the world with over 4.25 million CCTV cameras, one for every fifteen people[i]. All this data is stored digitally and securely online.

In the US, the situation is similar with the Patriot Act granting US enforcement agencies the same sort of powers.

But it's not just Government agencies that can find out what you do online. It's much more than that.

Social media websites such as Facebook and MySpace have a huge reach, with Facebook alone having around 120 million worldwide users[ii]. In the developed westernised economy there will be at least one user of social media who knows you, probably ten or more – and if you're under 30, you can double that figure.

And at some point, information will appear online about you.

The question is, will what appears online be complimentary? Will social media users be writing about how elegantly you were dressed and how articulate and interesting you were? Will what appears enhance your professional reputation?

Or will a less-than-complimentary description be accompanied by a photo of you slumped over your desk after a particularly heavy night out? Or with grease paint on your face as you follow your favourite sports team? Will there perhaps be a veiled reference to an alleged affair you might be having? Or a description of why you were made redundant in your last job?

Imagine a scenario where every bad decision you made or every indiscretion was opened up for all to see. Scary thought?

Welcome to the very connected world we now live in.

But there's more. Much more.

Take newspapers. Your local newspaper might have written a story about you, perhaps something worthwhile like your involvement with a local charity – or something less flattering like a drink-driving conviction. Old printed newspapers might simply become tomorrow's fish and chip wrapper, but now that newspapers have gone online you can expect your story to 'stick'. And it will stick – for years to come.

Or what about website forums? Most internet users will be members of one or more internet groups. It might be a forum on helping the blind or it might be a forum on something less savoury. However, the internet is not private

1.3   The concept of 'yesterdays news' is dead

and unless such forums are heavily ring-fenced with members-only access, the subject matter is there for all to see.

What about video sharing sites such as YouTube? YouTube, owned by Google, is one of the largest *search engines* in terms of website traffic. Visit it now, input your name and ask yourself: 'does what appears about me enhance or damage my reputation?'

Even if you don't have videos of yourself online, other people will certainly have taken photos of you and the copyright belongs to them, not you. Photo-sharing websites such as Flickr have enormous popularity and in November 2008, Flickr alone had three billion images publicly available to view.[iii] Given there are only six billion people alive, very soon almost everyone will have a photo of themselves somewhere on the web. The question is, are these photos of the type you would want your professional contacts – such as recruiters, your employer or your clients – to see?

REPUTATION ACTION

- ✔ Note down the websites you interact with most. These could be sites where you write your own blog, or sites you use to comment on other people's blogs, social network sites on which you talk to friends, or job sites where you upload your CV and application details.

- ✔ Now write down what you do on those sites that involves creating your own content. The content you upload could be your opinion, it could relate to your personal interests, fun stuff, or may even be images of your holidays. Maybe you pose or respond to business related questions, or create searches targeting new job opportunities.

- ✔ Whatever this information is, by creating it, you are already laying the foundations of managing your personal reputation.

1.4   Your world is becoming more and more connected

The world's biggest library at your fingertips

So far, we've talked about the information you might find when you're using a computer. But increasingly, the internet itself is converging with mobiles and other communications devices to the point where gadgets such as the iPhone and BlackBerry, are becoming ubiquitous must-have digital applications in themselves.

Using these devices people are able to search for you in real time, in the pub, in the boardroom, on the train, even on a plane. It might sound like something out of Ridley Scott's 1982 film *Blade Runner*, but it's here now.

In the near future there will be as many internet searches conducted on the fly, using mobiles and PDAs, as there will be on computers.

Consider an even more fantastic future when facial recognition from these mobile devices pulls out all the information on you that is available, in real time, and organises it and presents it to you in the palm of your hand. It's not that far away.

So with the internet readily accessible on your iPhone, your BlackBerry or your PDA, everyone is effectively carrying round the combined contents of every library in the world, all within the palms of their hands. And that library contains information about you.

To manage your reputation effectively, you need to understand why anyone would want to find out about you.

And by understanding what people want to find out about you, you are taking the first step to being in control of what they find when they search for you.

You can then proceed to thinking about whether you are:

- Promoting yourself;
- Protecting your reputation; or
- Connecting with like-minded professionals.

It's probably a combination of all of the above. Being in control of your personal reputation can only benefit you; it will help with job offers, new customers, or impressing your current employer. People want to know about you, so give them what they want.

You're either in control or you're not

We've now established that the internet is all-pervasive and affects almost every area of your life, the situation now facing you is this:

Your personal reputation is in serious danger if you don't look after it.

If you are not in control of what people find when they search for you online you are missing out on a world of opportunities.

The implications are profound. If you're not in control of the personal information that appears about you online, then you are at the mercy of other people's descriptions, opinions and even photographs and videos.

If you let others put up all the information about you and your life then at the very least you need to make sure they have an interest in promoting you. Better still, don't leave it to chance and begin promoting yourself first.

In our current combative economic climate your reputation is your competitive advantage. What is more important that looking after your good name? If you want your audience to take notice of what you have to offer and can show you understand the value of your own 'brand', you are much better placed to take advantage of the next opportunity that comes along. Your reputation has a real monetary value, don't underestimate it and take control.

Why personal reputation matters

So what you ask? Why does it matter if my life is laid bare on the internet? After all, I don't have anything to hide...

The reason is this: when people who are important to you want to know about a new job candidate or want to find out if a recommended person or service is trustworthy, they will go to one of the leading search engines – such as Google, AOL, Yahoo, Bing or Ask Jeeves – and type in the name of that person.

They will then formulate an opinion based on the first page or two of the *search engine results*. Forget about pages three onwards as research shows that people only read the first page of results and perhaps the second but rarely the third page or more[iv].

The bottom line is that people use search engines to research other people. Someone, somewhere has 'Googled' your name.

HERE'S WHY THIS MATTERS:

1. Prospective employers will research you on the internet rather than rely purely on your CV, particularly if this is your first job.

2. Your current employer will want to know if you are trustworthy and not someone who discusses sensitive company information on social media sites, blogs or websites.

3. New clients or customers will look at what is written on the internet about you (not just about your company) before making a purchasing decision.

You can't escape these facts. As we move deeper into a ubiquitous digital age, search engines will become even more important than they are now.

The question is, do you know what already appears about you? Do you have any control over what people see when they search for your name? If not, now is the time to start.

▲▲ Be yourself. Everybody else is already taken. ▼▼

Oscar Wilde

Generations X, Y and Z

This situation is even more extreme if you are under 30 years of age.

Why? The internet only became viable as a mass communication tool in the mid-to-late nineties and it is only since then that the internet has become an important part of people's everyday lives. For people under 30, therefore, all of their adult lives will have developed in tandem with the internet and digital communications such as mobile phones. Text messaging, instant messaging and the ability to be always connected to their peers, friends and social groups are the driving force for a big part of this age group's leisure and learning activities.

The problem, however, is that young teenagers and young adults will have used the internet predominantly as a social tool – showing warts and all.

This is fine, up to a point, but what happens when teenagers and young adults look for work? Many employers now only pass a cursory glance at a CV and instead simply undertake a Google search and study what appears about that person. Far more can be gleaned from an internet search than a CV.

Therefore, it's critical that young people know how to manage their online profile and are on top of their personal reputation; otherwise it could damage their career before it's even started.

If you're over the age of 30 and a business owner, executive or professional, don't be fooled into thinking these same rules don't apply to you. In fact, the reverse is true. If you have been moderately successful in any way, there will be a reference to you on the internet – perhaps alongside some rather drunken pictures or revealing indiscretions you'd rather remained hidden.

Even if you can't be found through an internet search, that's not good news either. In fact, if you don't exist online you are effectively invisible. Either way – you want to make sure that when a prospective employer or customer searches for you they only find the information you want them to see about you. Otherwise, you could be putting yourself at a huge disadvantage in the job market.

WHO WOULD YOU OFFER A JOB TO?

▸ A candidate who came across well in person and, when you searched for them, you found several professional blog entries, social media profiles, and a well-designed and informative website.

OR

▸ A candidate who came across equally well in person, but when you did a search engine query you discovered various revealing holiday snaps and inappropriate language, showing at best some of their 'fun' personality or, at worst, just plain bad judgement in caring for their personal reputation.

Now for the good news

Whether you are aware of it or not, you are already an expert in personal reputation management.

You probably carefully select your clothes and wear what feels most in line with your own personal identity. For some people that might mean haute couture, for others the high street or market.

Where it's bought is not the issue, what's important is that the clothes reflect your personal identity; you are happy with the image you are projecting to others and you feel good wearing them.

It's the same for personal grooming. You will have your favourite hair stylist, and your favourite grooming or beauty products and perfumes. You will have your favourite face creams and moisturisers.

All of these play an important part in presenting to the world a particular image of you. In short, you are managing your personal reputation.

And it's not just the way you visually present yourself to the world either.

Whether you know it or not, your personal mannerisms, style of communication and body language will also portray you in the image that you would like to be seen – and in your professional life, this is even more important.

REPUTATION THOUGHT

- What facets of your personality are you consistently projecting? Are you friendly? Efficient? Dynamic? Do you get on with people?

- Begin thinking about how you are perceived and how it matches your professional aims and objectives. Managing your reputation online is about understanding your strengths as a person and using digital technology to amplify them.

Vocal tone, speed of delivery, accent, body posture and head movements are all cultivated – consciously or unconsciously – to present a certain image of yourself to the world. Much of this will be automatic or even subconscious behaviour – a bit like driving a car – but it will be carefully managed all the same.

Part of this will be based on pure survival instinct. For example, your accent will have evolved from an early age unconsciously to fit into the social grouping you belong to and the region where you grew up.

However, as basic survival needs such as shelter, clothing and housing have all been provided for in westernised economies, a more individualistic culture has arisen. With basic necessities met, people have striven to stand out in the cultures they belong to and greater emphasis has been placed on personal appearance, status and apparent wealth.

In short, more than at any other time in human history, people are paying serious attention to personal reputation management.

In effect, a person's own personal reputation is now his or her own brand, mirroring the development and cultivation of marketing brands in the commercial world.

Yes, some people put more importance on it than others – politicians for instance, where reputation is everything. But there is nobody on this planet that does not have a vested interest in personal reputation management, be they a CEO entertaining at a fine restaurant in New York or a graduate trying to stand out amongst thousands of other candidates.

REPUTATION ACTION

✔ Write down the names of three business personalities who have leveraged their personal reputation for commercial benefit. The media and technology savvy will have their own blogs, websites and feedback mechanisms in place to monitor, manage and control their reputations – and by default their companies' reputations.

✔ Here are two to get you started:
- **Richard Branson:** Adventurous, clever, operates outside the normal corporate convention. That sounds a bit like the Virgin brand doesn't it?

- **Steve Jobs:** Colourful, innovative, dynamic. Does that sound like a particular fruity computer brand you know?

Think about how these people have imposed their personalities onto their companies and successfully created space for themselves in a busy and competitive market. This formula applies equally to you. Give your target audience exactly what they want; be they customers or clients, a human resource manager or your current employer – and make it easy for them to understand what you have to offer. Say it and keep on saying it, and use the ubiquitous ability of the internet to spread your message clearly and consistently.

Personal reputation is essential for adaptation into the society you live in. The only people not interested in personal reputation management are those most likely to be on the very margins and fringes of society, although even they will have their own social codes and rules that they follow.

Reputation Case Study: British National Party members

This case study demonstrates the effect of private information – the type that a person would guard closely – suddenly becoming publicly available online, and the ramifications of this.

In November 2008, the entire 12,000 strong membership of the British National Party (BNP) was leaked and posted on an internet site. The BNP political party, while completely legal, is viewed in many quarters as an 'extremist far-right organisation' with its whites-only policy and a constitutional mandate to 'stem and reverse the tide of non-white immigration'[v].

Despite holding 0.7 per cent of the popular vote in the 2005 General Election, 100 UK councillors and a seat on the London Assembly, the party has always been severely marginalised in the UK media with acres of negative press.

When the BNP's membership list was leaked online, it was jumped upon by a gleeful media looking for sensational information about public figures or people they could turn into interesting stories.

They weren't disappointed: Cambridge University lecturers, radio presenters, doctors, vicars, social workers, anti-terror officers, policemen, and even Buckingham Palace staff, were found to have been on the membership list. As the UK's *Daily Mail*, remarked, "the list is not what the BNP members are supposed to be like. Instead of shaven-headed thugs, the membership list reveals a surprising number of professionals leading apparently respectful lives."[vi]

Suddenly, all these 'respectable' people had their reputations exposed online.

What was the effect? Let's see for ourselves:

Take Robin Hill, a musician and supposedly an official staff member of Leeds University. Google Robin's name, however, and the lead posting is his membership of the BNP[vii]. Furthermore, Leeds University quickly released a terse statement after the BNP membership data was leaked, saying he'd never been an officially registered member of staff but was in fact just a private tutor[viii]. His online reputation is now in tatters with his membership of the BNP fully exposed.

How about Reverend John Stanton of Rochford, Essex? Almost the entire first page of his Google listing is taken up by stories surrounding his BNP membership.

Then there is Arthur Nightingale,

Google™

Reverend John Stanton   [Search]   Advan Prefer

Search: ⦿ the web ◯ pages from the UK

Web

Church leader 'stupid' to sign up to the BNP (From Echo) 〔⇡〕〔✕〕
The **Rev John Stanton**, who was Lib Dem chairman of Rochford District Council in 1997,
admitted he was "stupid" for not knowing what the BNP really stood for ...
www.echo-news.co.uk/news/2159948.church_leader_stupid_to_sign_up_to_the_bnp/ - 62k -
Cached - Similar pages - ⊝

BNP **Reverend** Has Damascene Experience « Bartholomew's Notes on ... 〔⇡〕
1 Apr 2008 ... The **Rev John Stanton**, who was elected Lib Dem chairman of Rochford
District Council in 1997, is now the far-right party's organiser for the ...
barthsnotes.wordpress.com/2008/04/01/bnp-**reverend**-has-damascene-experience/ - 42k -
Cached - Similar pages - ⊝

Faces behind the BNP names | The Sun |News 〔⇡〕〔✕〕
20 Nov 2008 ... **Rev John Stanton**, 75. A VICAR named on the leaked BNP membership list
last night ... **Rev John Stanton**, 75, who runs the Rock Dene Christian ...
www.thesun.co.uk/sol/homepage/news/article1950736.ece - Similar pages - ⊝

1.5   Page 1 Google search results for "Reverend John Stanton"

Google™

Rod Lucas   [Search]   Advanced Search Preferences

Search: ⦿ the web ◯ pages from the UK

Web

ROD LUCAS.COM OFFICIAL SITE 〔⇡〕〔✕〕
This is the offical **Rod Lucas** web site. Catch up on all the latest programme news here.
www.rodlucas.com/ - 30k - Cached - Similar pages - ⊝

Rod Lucas dropped by TalkSPORT after BNP links emerge - Telegraph 〔⇡〕〔✕〕
19 Nov 2008 ... TalkSPORT radio station has lost its second DJ in a week after **Rod Lucas**
was one of the names on the leaked BNP members list.
www.telegraph.co.uk/news/uknews/3484612/**Rod-Lucas**-dropped-by-TalkSPORT-after-
BNP-links-emerge.html - Similar pages - ⊝

video: Radio DJ **Rod Lucas** axed after appearing on BNP membership ... 〔⇡〕〔✕〕
19 Nov 2008 ... A male police officer in Merseyside and a radio DJ are the first alleged BNP
members to face consequences after the far-right party's full ...
www.timesonline.co.uk/tol/news/uk/article5189610.ece - Similar pages - ⊝

Talksport DJ **Rod Lucas** fired after appearing on leaked BNP list ... 〔⇡〕〔✕〕
Talksport DJ **Rod Lucas** has been fired after appearing on a leaked list of alleged members of
the BNP.
www.mirror.co.uk/news/top-stories/2008/.../talksport-dj-**rod-lucas**-fired-after-appearing-

1.6   Page 1 Google search results for "Rod Lucas"

Cont. Reputation Case Study: British National Party Members

a senior engineer at Cambridge University. Type in 'Arthur Nightingale Cambridge University' and rather than a showcase of his academic credentials and achievements, almost the whole of the first page of his Google search results is dedicated to his BNP membership.

While the impact on private individuals was bad enough, the effect of the leak was even more devastating on well-known personalities.

Rod Lucas, the TalkSPORT radio DJ, was one of those named on the BNP's membership list. Despite claiming that his membership was for research purposes only, when his employers found out that he was a listed member he was dropped from the radio station altogether[ix]. He is now setting up an English news station in Spain, away from all the UK controversy[x].

What he will find, however, is that he cannot escape his online personal reputation. In fact, when you type his name into the Yahoo! search engine it doesn't showcase his various prestigious radio awards but highlights his membership of the BNP and subsequent sacking from TalkSPORT.

But worse still, these search engine results will last for years, severely harming his, and the other reputations of the 12,000 individuals involved, for a long time to come.

These examples demonstrate firsthand the impact of the power of the internet on your personal reputation.

Whatever you think of someone's political views, what these case studies also expose is how a slight on your personality – whether true or untrue – can be magnified and enlarged online for everyone to see. This scenario equally applies to you. A rival business or job applicant could defame you or your company by spreading rumours about the problems with a new product or the HR director's past indiscretions.

In a very short space of time all the respectable aspects of you and your life are suddenly relegated in importance and the negative results appear on search engines for everyone to see.

Understanding the value of your personal reputation helps you take back control and ensure you are ready when negative comments or content threaten your professional or personal life.

Why personal reputation management must extend into the digital sphere

The digital sphere is now where your reputation battle will be fought, and where information, contacts, support and opportunities are waiting for you. What baffles internet experts, however, is why some people spend unimaginable hours on carefully crafting their external 'offline' image yet pay no attention to their online profile.

This is a mistake.

The online world is growing exponentially. Everything we do is being recorded, filmed and held as raw data on vast super computers – from what we buy and where we bought it to what activities we engage in and when we engage in them.

Basically, unless you live off the grid somewhere in the Outer Hebrides, communicating only by post and purchasing simple items with cash, then your life is far more 'digitised' than you could ever believe.

Everything we do is recorded and stored digitally.

Your interests, the clubs you join, the jobs you have had are all available to be searched for online.

While the majority of this information is stored privately and securely by commercial enterprises and Government agencies, some of this information is also publicly available.

Add to this the sheer volume of generally available information such as social media websites, forums, blogs and so on, and the information available about you is unprecedented and growing all the time.

◢◢ If you don't show up in a Google search for your name or product, you don't exist ▮▮

William Arruda – Branding Expert

And at the same time, somebody somewhere could be searching for someone with your skills or attributes right now, so it is in your commercial interest to manage what they find.

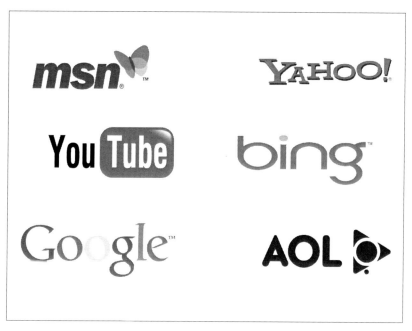

You've been searched

Personal information is accessed online primarily – in fact almost exclusively – using search engines. While Google is the world's most popular search engine, there are many others that are also important including AOL, Live Search, Yahoo! and YouTube. There are also hundreds of other niche search engines that register millions of hits each month – in one month alone in 2008, eBay registered 434 million searches while Craigslist users logged 335 million searches[xi].

Many of these searches on the niche sites would have been commercially oriented – holiday searches, product searches, research and general information, for example. However, a significant volume of general searches would have been personal searches – people, employers, or customers looking for personal information on other people.

Where it gets very interesting is when you start factoring in the search engines on social media websites. Social media sites such as Facebook and MySpace register 186 million and 585 million searches respectively each month[xii]. And searches on these sites are almost all individually-oriented. That is, people searching for information on other people.

What's not in doubt is that each month, there are billions of searches across a variety of search engines. Most importantly, many of these searches are searches about other people. People like you.

Smile, you're on video

In 2006, Google thought highly enough of video-sharing website YouTube to purchase it for $1.65bn[xiii].

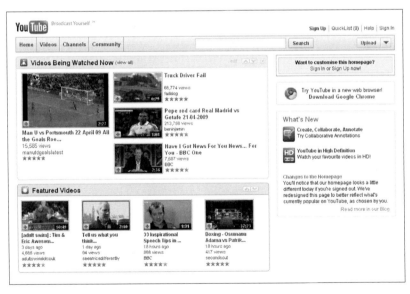

1.8   YouTube

Far and away the biggest video-sharing service in the world, Google now includes YouTube video clips amongst the text listings of its search engine results. It demonstrates how video is becoming an increasingly important element of reputation management. It is an excellent, and low-cost way to showcase who you are and what you can offer. A simple camcorder or high quality phone camera can record a mission statement and contact details for your current status – whether you are looking for a job or new business opportunities. It can be set up and uploaded directly to YouTube in a matter of minutes. Product reviews, industry video blogs, information about your business or demos for new services, the list is endless.

This now means that your uploaded YouTube video clip will appear on Google searches and is accessible to your target audience. However this immediacy also has its drawbacks – others can post less welcome video clips of you with the same amount of speed. A clip of you tied to a lamppost on your stag weekend, or out on the town after one too many drinks.

What this means

If you are not in control of your personal online profile, then you are taking a big risk.

The big question for you is this: will the information posted about you work in your best interest? If you're looking for a new job or negotiating an important business contract, will what is written enhance your prospects or ruin them?

You wouldn't let other people choose your hairstyle, decide what you wear, how you talk and act. Why then would you let others have control over your online persona?

Your reputation is important and you need to be in control of all aspects of it.

This is why it's vital that you are in control of your online profile and your digital reputation. Soon it will be as important as your offline reputation and, in time, both will merge together with no obvious delineation.

You can do something about it.

We have outlined the importance of personal reputation management and why your online image is as important as your offline image.

We have also shared the bad news that you are probably not in control about what is written or videoed about you online.

But you don't have to leave it to chance. You can take action and present to the world the personal image that best represents you. You can take control of your personal reputation management.

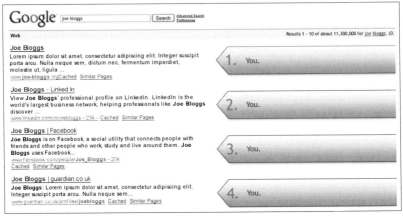

1.9   What do you find when you search for your name?

WHAT CAN THIS BOOK DO FOR YOU?

- Show you how to protect and promote your personal reputation online.

- Give you a competitive advantage in today's tough economic climate, whether you are a graduate, professional or business owner.

- Tell the major search engines how to find you.

- Show you how to use social media to your advantage.

- Deliver a better understanding to the background of personal reputation management and explain why it matters so much.

- Show you how to clean up your digital profile.

- Outline a set of actions and techniques that demonstrate how you can manage, maintain and enhance your online profile no matter what has been written (or videoed) about you in the past – or will be in the future.

- Put simply, it will show you how to begin managing your online personal reputation properly and professionally. So you can get that job, win that new client or secure that new piece of business.

- Help you take control of your primary asset: You.

Up next: The history of reputation management

2

A brief history of reputation

"Character is like a tree and a reputation like a shadow.
The shadow is what we think of it; the tree is the real thing."
Abraham Lincoln

Human beings have always been conscious of their reputation. In fact, there has never been a time in history when a person's reputation hasn't been visible. This makes it important.

Even during the Stone Age, 40,000 years ago, our earliest ancestors tailored their own clothing and finely decorated it with ornaments to enhance their personal image[i]. Personal reputation and image were so important to them that it gave birth to perhaps the world's oldest manufacturing industry: jewellery.

Our ancestors tried to further preserve their reputation in the form of cave paintings and drawings. Cave paintings can be found all over the world – 350 such caves have been discovered in France and Spain alone – and often depict scenes of wild animals, hunting and various forms of social interaction.

Many indigenous peoples from around the world still continue to produce artistic works today. Some commentators have even suggested that people's personal websites are simply a hi-tech form of cave art through which humans convey their feelings, aspirations and reputation.

2.1 A cave painting in Algeria (Photographed by Patrick Gruban)

A matter of physical survival

In those days, of course, an individual's personal reputation management was all about survival.

Why?

If tribal members failed to look like other members of their tribe, they risked misidentification and possible death. At the very least, they risked exclusion from their tribe.

Tribe members, therefore, needed to look like other members of their tribe in order to fit in.

Such was the importance of fitting into a social group, tribe members rarely – if ever – considered their own individuality. Instead, tribes managed their own personal reputations as part of a social grouping.

This situation still exists today as anthropologists investigating the furthest reaches of the Amazon or Papua New Guinea consistently find tribal members showing a high level of group conformity. The reason for this is clear: in tribal culture, group belonging was – and still is – essential for personal safety.

Physical survival becomes emotional survival

Group conformity is still important in modern culture with fashion, design, hairstyles, voice mannerisms and speech phrases still very much governed by societal trends.

In fact, whether you realise it or not, many of your personal habits and preferences will be unconsciously based on fitting in to the society in which you live.

The moment you 'stand out from the crowd', you are likely to feel threatened and experience the same survival instincts that governed Stone Age man. While your physical security might no longer be endangered, your emotional security and sense of belonging could feel under threat.

Belonging, or social identity, is a central aspect of how we feel about ourselves. In fact, it is our membership of particular groupings of individuals that probably has the single greatest influence on our sense of personal identity and self esteem. By fitting into a particular group or groups, we feel accepted and valued, which in turn give us confidence and a feeling of wellbeing about our place in the world.[ii]

My dear dear lord, The purest treasure mortal times afford is spotless reputation. That away, Men are but gilded loam or painted clay.

William Shakespeare

The internet's growth is in no small measure due to its ability to answer this basic human need – it is a place where people naturally form groups with shared or common interests. For this reason, the internet is now essential to many people's sense of connection.

This is why your online profile is so vital, not just for your reputation but also your mental wellbeing – both are strongly interdependent because feeling accepted within society is psychologically important.

To that end, it is crucial that your online profile assists you in adapting to the society within which you live and doesn't work against you by highlighting those aspects of yourself that should remain private.

The beginning of world trade

With the domestication of wild animals and advances in basic movement of goods, prehistoric people began to carry loads over greater distances. Extensive grassland provided fertile grazing, especially in the steppes of Asia, and cultural exchanges and trade developed rapidly between Asia, Europe and Africa.

Chief amongst these were the silk routes, which were not only conduits for silk, but also other products such as musk, rubies, diamonds, pearls and even rhubarb.[iii] These trade routes extended over 5,000 miles and simultaneously spread knowledge, ideas, cultures and, unfortunately, disease.

Suddenly a whole new group of individuals arose – merchants – who quickly established themselves as a new and important social class.

The merchants' personal reputations were vital in allowing them to trade, travel and hold key positions in society. A bad reputation for delivery of damaged goods or bad quality merchandise often ended in death.

For the first time, personal reputation transcended issues of mere physical survival and became instrumental in allowing people to interact and trade with each other successfully.

Today, personal reputation may not carry the threat of physical danger, but for personal and business growth it is as vitally important as it was 2,000 years ago.

In fact it's even more important.

Why? The background of individuals and companies is laid bare on the internet for anyone to research, and worldwide communications are instantaneous. People can find out everything about you online in seconds and make immediate judgements based on what they discover.

If you are engaged in any type of commercial activity, it's therefore vital that your online reputation enhances your ability to do business rather than diminishes it. This is increasingly true of individuals and the reputations they project to the world. As technology becomes cheaper and gains mass-market appeal, people are offered greater and more co-ordinated experiences. Brands are becoming truly individual – to make the necessary 'human' connection - and at the same time individuals are becoming brands, mimicking successful businesses in communicating consistent messages, crisis management and promotion in the personal sense.

Social mobility

Merchants were instrumental in developing social mobility because people, for the first time, were able to live and trade in different regions worldwide, allowing new social groupings to form.

This has its comparisons to today, where social mobility is still primarily based on work and business, as seen in the mass movement of people recently between Eastern Europe and the European Union.

However, the internet has now become an additional key influence in modern social mobility. New business opportunities, trade openings, recruitment notices and general news are circulated around the world in seconds making social mobility faster than before.

Just as quickly, however, business partners are able to reference new contacts, clients and partners in the blink of an eye by accessing their details online.

This is why your online reputation must protect and enhance you, otherwise it won't be just your business potential that is affected – your social mobility might be critically impaired as well.

2.2 Early merchants in pursuit of social mobility

Merchants and Empire

Commerce on the silk road was a major factor in the development of the great civilisations of Babylon (1728 BC), Egypt (1600 BC), Greece (800 BC), Persian Empires (728 BC), China (2500 BC) and Rome (509 BC), and in many respects it helped lay the foundations for the modern world.

Commerce and trade underpinned these great empires, with merchants influencing and shaping the culture of each society.

Within these civilisations, however, a person's status was worth more than a person's individual reputation.

This is an important distinction to make. Usually granted through birth and genealogy rather than wealth, such status allowed members of the elite classes to behave outside normal societal restrictions and get away with it.

In short, because individual status could rarely be threatened, reputation was less important.

In *A Short History of the World*, HG Wells describes the first two centuries of the Roman Empire as "slave states... built upon thwarted wills, stifled intelligence and crippled and perverted desires."[iv] These desires included rampant pursuit of adventure (for most Romans with leisure and money) and barbarous personal pursuits, like watching human death at the Coliseum as a means of relaxation.

These desires would rarely threaten a person's reputation – exposure of a Roman's deviant behaviour did not reflect on his ability to govern, nor did it usually terminate a political career. In fact, so long as his behaviour "didn't frighten the horses", a Roman's progress either socially or politically would not be impeded.[v]

Antony (of Antony and Cleopatra fame), for example, was exhibited as a boy for sale in a woman's toga, the outfit of a prostitute. Despite this, he later became triumvir and would have been the ruler of the world had he not lost the Battle of Actium with Cleopatra.

This is in contrast with today where even presidents, kings and queens have to behave within clearly defined social parameters or risk being ousted.

However, Antony didn't have Facebook, YouTube or Flickr to contend with. We do. This is why maintaining your online personal reputation is so important.

2.3 *Antony and Cleopatra.* Oil panting by Lawrence Alma-Tadema (1885)

2.4 An engraving of a printer using the early Gutenberg press during the 15th century

Your status no longer offers protection.

In today's vibrant and connected society, your ability to enhance your reputation and to correct any online slights on your character is a great leveller. Anybody can influence your profile if you choose to interact on the internet; anybody can comment favourably or negatively. It is up to you, therefore, to use this level playing field to your advantage. Being up to speed with business competitors, other job candidates or peers means being switched on to exploiting the digital technology revolution.

The advent of printing and literacy

It wasn't until the invention of the printing press in the 15th century by Johannes Gutenberg that a groundbreaking rupture in the status quo occurred – words could be printed and distributed for the first time.

This created a revolution in literacy and allowed people to relay their personal reputation in a completely new form (just like the internet has done today).

Two hundred years later, printing was sufficiently advanced to see the creation of newspapers. The UK's first newspaper was the *London Gazette*, while in the US, *Public Occurrences* launched in 1690.

The actual news, however, was frequently highly selective: the ruling elite and governments used newspapers as ways to publish accounts of wars or events that portrayed them in a favourable light to the public.

The emergence of newspaper dailies

It was only with the emergence of mass-market newspapers such as *The Times of London* in the 18th century that the landscape for personal reputation management changed forever.

For the first time, news and information could be relayed quickly to a significant percentage of the population on a daily basis.

Even up until the last few decades, however, many newspapers refused to impinge on a person's personal reputation. Part of this was for legal reasons due to slander and libel laws. Another reason was the great store placed on personal privacy and journalistic integrity within the press.

In addition, the ruling class in many countries were also the very same people owning the newspapers, and they helped ensure that friends and acquaintances were never portrayed in a negative light in the press.

THE LONDON GAZETTE

Published by Authority.

From Monday, Septemb 3, to Monday, Septemp 10, 1666.

Whitehall, Sept. 8.

THE ordinary course of this paper having been interrupted by a sad and lamentable accident of Fire lately hapned in the City of *London*: it hath been thought fit for satisfying the minds of so many of His Majesties good Subjects who must needs be concerned for the Issue of so great an accident, to give this short, but true Accompt of it. On the second instant, at one of the clock in the Morning, there hapned to break out, a sad in deplorable Fire in *Pudding-lane*, neer *New Fish-*

Church, neer *Holborn-bridge*, *Pie-corner*, *Aldersgate*, *Cripple-gate*, neer the lower end of *Coleman-street*, at the end of *Basin-hall-street* by the *Postern* at the upper end of *Bishopsgate-street* and *Leadenhall-street*, at the *Standard* in *Cornhill* at the church in *Fenchurch street*, neer *Cloth-workers Hall* in *Mincing-lane*, at the middle of *Mark-lane*, and at the *Tower-dock*.

On Thursday by the blessing of God it was wholly beat down and extinguished. But so as that Evening it unhappily burst out again a fresh at the *Temple*, by the falling of some sparks (as is supposed) upon a Pile of Wooden buildings; but his Royal Highness who watched there that vvhole

2.5   The London Gazette front page from 1666, reporting on the Fire of London

This meant that people in the public eye, such as politicians, never needed to worry about the exposure of their personal reputation to the general public or their peers.

What a contrast to today where a person with any level of public fame is subject to intense scrutiny both on and offline. There are also fewer boundaries to the stories written, with salacious details often leapt upon and quickly given wider exposure.

This is why it's imperative that you protect and ring fence your personal reputation by carefully managing, it and are aware of the common danger areas. It is a powerful incentive knowing that when someone searches for you on the internet, they are as likely to find negative or damaging content as they are to see positive information if you are not in control of the results.

King Edward and Mrs Simpson

Journalistic values changed in the early part of the 20th century, around the time that the story of King Edward and Mrs Simpson's love tryst was leaked, causing a sensation and constitutional crisis in the English monarchy. Despite both the King and government pressuring the British media to maintain silence, it was left to *The New York Journal* to break the story "King will wed Wally".

This eventually led to Edward abdicating from the throne in 1936 and the event was one of the earliest examples of how newspapers could break someone's personal reputation – even one belonging to a King.

It was also one of the earliest and most graphic examples of how a person's status, no matter how elevated, could be destroyed by their personal reputation.

It was at this point in history that a person's own individual reputation became of paramount importance and superseded family, status and power.

The advent of liberalism: 1960s onwards

The Sixties witnessed an unprecedented evolution in society, as many facets of society fundamentally changed – driven by the sexual revolution, liberalisation of music and art, the civil rights movement, and general unshackling of restrictive social codes of behaviour – all of which led to a sea change in human values.

Coinciding with this was the proliferation of media and the emergence of modern day television as the world's preferred medium of entertainment, first in black and white and subsequently in colour.

TV changed the influence of the media forever as it put the media at the heart of people's daily lives – in their own front rooms.

The late Sixties and Seventies also saw the rise of the tabloid newspapers. Papers such as Germany's *Bild-Zeitung*, the UK's *The Sun* newspaper and the US' *National Enquirer* rose in popularity (and continue to sell millions of copies today). Written in a sensational style, tabloids started to give far more prominence to celebrities, sports, crime stories, and salacious gossip.

The media slowly moved en masse towards a more populist platform where often the lowest common denominator triumphed.

Individuals were suddenly more exposed to the whims of the media, which delighted in the new-found liberalism in exposing every indiscretion and peccadillo.

Growth of the internet

Then, as if the changes in the latter half of the 20th century weren't enough, we witnessed the birth of the internet.

From humble beginnings as a scientific and military tool, the internet has seen explosive growth from obscurity to ubiquity in little over ten years.

Bill Gates, Chairman of Microsoft and a prominent player in the development of the internet, wrote in his book *Business @ the Speed of Thought* that in 1995 only 50 per cent of companies used email. Who would have imagined email would become almost ubiquitous over the following few years?

What started off as basic browsing of single text pages and simple messaging transformed into more sophisticated user applications, such as email and ecommerce. However, it wasn't really until after the dotcom bust of 2000 to 2002 that the internet flourished to embrace many aspects of individual's lives.

These applications – *RSS feeds*, the mobile internet, *WiFi*, broadband television, GPS navigation, digital music, webcams, instant messaging and social media to name a few – have meant that the internet has now infiltrated all our lives on many levels. Rather than being a separate standalone tool, the internet now plays an essential role in many of our key daily interactions.

Fast forward to the present day and devices such as the iPhone are converging many of the internet's key functions onto a single, mobile device. These devices allow users to interact with the internet wherever they are, and offer functions as varied as listening to music, taking photographs, phoning, emailing, GPS satellite navigation and ecommerce.

We can't do without the internet now in order to function in our daily lives.

This is why managing your online reputation is more important than ever because the boundaries between online and offline are merging into one.

In the blink of an eye

These sudden changes in personal reputation management have occurred in the blink of an eye.

People and society in general have simply not had the time to come to terms with the importance of an individual's reputation and how easily it can be damaged.

This has left individuals feeling lost and helpless in their ability to maintain their personal reputation, especially online. They haven't been told how critical it is and more importantly, no guidance has been given as to how to manage it.

Conversely, most people still don't understand how easy it is to take control of their individual reputations and to use these new connections to enhance their economic goals and objectives. All it takes is an understanding of its importance, and the proactive development of a reputation strategy to help develop and maintain a consistent professional image.

We believe personal reputation management is now fundamental to our society, we foresee a time in the near future when reputation management classes will be taught at schools and universities.

Reputation Case Study: Lord Peter Mandelson

This case study highlights the dangers of any online stories that might be written about you – stories that might not be considered indiscretions, but which would certainly contain facts you'd probably prefer remained hidden.

The case study in question involves Lord Peter Mandelson, UK Secretary of State for Business, Enterprise & Regulatory Reform.

Mandelson hasn't enjoyed the best relationship with the British media during his time in power. With nicknames such as Lord Sleaze and Prince of Darkness, the media watch his every step and move, particularly online[vi].

Here's why:

In 2008 a relatively unknown political newspaper called the *UK Column* uncovered a story about Peter Mandelson's domain name **www.petermandelson.com**. When anyone tried to visit the site, they were instead directed to a completely different website called NLP Connections, owned by a person named Chris Morris.

NLP, otherwise known as *Neuro-Linguistic Programming*, is a widely known and respected method of interpersonal communication,

which is used across many sectors of society[vii]. However, NLP also has a reputation for being modelled on "hypnotic suggestion" and dangerous "manipulation", earning it a chequered reputation in some quarters[viii].

Chris Morris refers to himself as "interested in the field of hypnosis and as a speechwriter, I studied the language in thousands of speeches and began to notice more and more that the most persuasive politicians use many of the same language patterns that hypnotists use, and I became curious about that."[ix]

So should we infer from the site confusion that the man known as Lord of Sleaze is a master hypnotist? Did Mandelson employ a hypnotist to write his speeches? Who knows, but it is rather odd that Mandelson's own domain name is registered to a hypnotist and NLP trainer.

At the very least one would assume there was some connection between them, especially as Chris Morris is a

Cont. Reputation Case Study: Lord Peter Mandelson

2.6   Peter Mandelson at the European Parliament, 2004

teacher of hypnosis and NLP, and runs workshops and private sessions on the use of these techniques for political purposes.

When certain enquiries were made as to the connection between Mandelson and Morris, Mandelson's own Parliamentary office never replied, and Chris Morris' website no longer appears when you type in Mandelson's domain name.

This is a classic example of how you have to be very careful in every aspect of your online dealings, not just your Google profile but also your own private domain name and website registration(s) and hosting.

One mistake and it's out in public across the web.

KEY LEARNINGS FROM THIS CHAPTER

■ There has never been a point in history when a person's reputation hasn't been important, from Prehistoric times to the present day.

■ Conformity is still a primary motivating force today, as is group belonging. Both are fundamental drivers in the growth of the internet as people establish their own networks and groupings in order to forge their own social identity.

■ Social identity is a fundamental aspect of what it is to be human, as is emotional security and self esteem – the internet satisfies these emotional needs on many different levels. Hence, its power and influence in today's society.

■ The beginning of world trade and the birth of the merchant class meant that personal reputations became essential for people to be able to trade with each other. This is the same today except that people's reputations are now available online 24/7.

■ During the great Empires, people's reputations were superseded by status. This has now changed and even Kings can be forced to abdicate if their reputation becomes tarnished.

■ The invention of the printing press started a revolution in literacy and the circulation of ideas. The creation of newspapers accelerated this process, while the inventions of TV and radio meant that today's media is all encompassing and comes at us from every angle instantaneously as news happens.

■ The internet has merely compounded this process and people are under more scrutiny than ever before with their every move analysed and put online.

- The internet has become ubiquitous, multi-functional and is converging onto single devices such as the iPhone. It has become essential to many areas of our lives.

- The online and offline worlds are merging. The management of your online personal reputation, therefore, has many ramifications across every aspect of your life.

Up next: Everyone's famous now ▷

3

Everyone's famous now

You are public property

With the advent of newspaper tabloids and commercial broadcasting in the 1960s, the mainstream media started to embrace popular culture.

This was partly due to commercial pressures whereby advertising revenue was tied to newspaper sales and TV viewings, therefore, the more popular the media, the bigger the advertising profits.

It was also due to the need for more editorial content. As the mainstream media became increasingly fragmented through an exponential rise in the number of broadcasters and publishers, the need for editorial content also grew.

Both factors have driven the media to adopt a popular platform in an attempt to appeal to as many people as possible. This has spawned the birth of celebrity culture as famous individuals capture people's imaginations, with celebrities either assuming the mantle of society's role models or scapegoats.

Over time, famous people have increasingly become public property as the sheer volume of attention lavished on them from the media grows every year. Celebrities have replaced community leaders and politicians as the nation's inspirational figures. Everyone wants to know what everybody else is doing and why they are doing it. Even more important than TV and print in fuelling this is the internet, where celebrity (and business, political and economic) news is continually breaking, and people can find the latest real-time updates.

Celebrity culture has grown rapidly

Celebrity culture has grown so fast that there are simply not enough high profile people to fill the acres of newspapers or miles of films. Such has been the demand for gossip and lifestyle content that broadcasters and newspapers have branched out to include many lesser known individuals who are only famous for being, well, famous.

In the UK, the best-selling women's magazines in 1959 were *Woman*, *Woman's Realm*, *Woman's Own* and *Woman's Weekly* – titles that focused on a woman's lifestyle, giving practical advice and tips[i].

Fast forward to today, and the top UK titles are *OK*, *Closer*, *Chat* and *Heat*. These titles contain little practical lifestyle advice and are instead more focused on celebrity gossip and personal trivia with a sensationalist bent.[ii]

It's not just magazines either. Most modern TV shows have introduced an element of celebrity to jazz them up.

'What's this got to do with me?' you might ask.

Everything.

Society's values are focused on exposing and elevating celebrity.

If you are not famous it doesn't matter, because if society is fixated on people's lives and lifestyles at a macro level, it follows that your life will become of more interest at a micro level – to people within your own social and work circles.

Reputation Case Study: Pete Townshend

This example looks at how online stories, particularly those of a scandalous or salacious nature, tend to sit high in Google rankings and can 'stick' for years.

His reputation at the upper echelons of popular music is peerless and his name rightly sits alongside such greats as Paul McCartney, Dave Gilmour, Jimmy Page, Robert Plant and other UK rock legends.

In 2003, however, he was cautioned by the police, following a four-month investigation into accusations that he accessed a paedophile website[iii]. The singer/guitarist argued that he had paid to access the Landslide website for research purposes in his campaign against all forms of pornography.[iv]

Despite only warranting a caution, he was severely criticised by the police who said: "It is not a defence to access these images for research or out of curiosity,"[v] and promptly placed him on the UK Sex Offenders Register for five years.

The NCH children's charity also heavily criticised the singer and released a statement saying, "It is not an acceptable defence and it only helps keep the child porn industry going."[vi]

And what has been the effect on Pete Townshend's online reputation? Type

3.1 Pete Townshend in concert with The Who, 2005

his name into Google's search engine and amongst the 1.5 million entries, his caution for accessing a paedophile site is ranked as the seventh biggest story.

You can't miss it... even now, six years later.

Pete Townshend's case study highlights the fact that any indiscretions – be they criminal, political, financial, sexual or anything considered to be noteworthy – will go online and they will stay for years.

3.2 Popular 'reality' talent shows

Everyone's a celebrity!

As society's values have filtered down and infused every level of our nation's culture, celebrity has branched out to ordinary individuals – people like you and me.

Talent shows such as *The X Factor* and *Britain's Got Talent* are all based on discovering latent talent amongst ordinary members of the public. These shows have been a worldwide phenomenon, spawning dozens of national variations.

The meteoric broadcasting rise of shows such as *The X Factor* has, in good part, been due to a gleeful national press who have covered every instalment of the talent shows and investigated and occasionally exposed the contestants.

For example, feisty singer Rachel Hylton, one of the contestants in the 2008 *X Factor*, was exposed by a British tabloid newspaper for living on £91.85 a week in unemployment state benefits while appearing on the show.[vii]

All of these celebrity TV formats are based on elevating talented members of the public and either glorifying them or shaming them.

They demonstrate more than ever the importance of keeping your personal reputation intact and managing it carefully, because in today's society, everybody is a celebrity.

TV goes voyeuristic

A shadowy side of the cult of celebrity has been the growth of voyeurism encapsulated by TV shows such as *Big Brother* and *The Jerry Springer Show*, both international TV sensations rolled out across dozens of countries worldwide.

Much of the success of these types of shows is the way they focus on exposing the hidden and dysfunctional sides of someone's personal reputation.

They have normalised the wrecking of a person's character and reputation for not conforming to society's expectations and codes of behaviour.

Just as importantly, they have helped bring the cult of celebrity down to the scale of the ordinary person.

Today, everyone is a celebrity.
Today everyone's personal reputation is considered fair game.
But here's the catch:

Today, your personal reputation is available online 24/7, 365 days a year.

This is why it is essential you safeguard and nurture your online personal reputation carefully. You need to be aware of what's being said about you.

Online nightmare

As people become fixated with each other, a whole generation of internet sites have emerged that focus on ordinary people and their inadequacies.

One such example is the website **www.dontdatehimgirl.com**, a top-ranking internet portal for women, with information on everything from how to find a great guy to boosting one's self-esteem.

It sounds helpful except that the site, with one million subscribers, also specialises in allowing women to post comments about men they've dated – particularly the ones who possibly should be given a wide berth.

Imagine if a malicious woman wants to take revenge on an ex-boyfriend because a relationship hasn't worked out? Now she can post a lengthy diatribe against him and also enlist her friends to help her.

When the unfortunate man begins dating again, any new dates might run a mile if they Google him and he appears on this website with a long list of derogatory comments attached to his name.

3.3 The dontdatehimgirl.com homepage

Can **www.dontdatehimgirl.com** prevent abuses of trust? No. It just asks for honesty and integrity when posting.[viii] However, given that the website is a site where "women go to bitch and warn other women about the losers they have dated including photos of the offending men, and comments about their sexual prowess,"[ix] the prospect of a fair hearing is slight.

Does this defamation appear on Yahoo!, Google and other search engines?

Yes.

Or what about the website **www.ripofftipoff.net**? This government-run site specialises in tipping off members of the public about dubious business practices. This is a good idea but only if all the people posting stories have integrity. In the event of a legitimate dispute, is it fair to have the details spread all over the internet?

Disagreements, quarrels and feuds are now going public over the internet.

Even worse, if someone '*Googles*' (*See Googling*) you, these arguments are available for all to see.

And if that wasn't enough, these stories will continue to appear long after any disagreements have been resolved.

Amateur media springs into existence

The internet has given rise to a huge number of groups, networks and communities, for almost every subject and cause imaginable.

Within these groups, there are leaders, influencers, originators, critics and followers, all with their own personal opinions and agendas. They are 'celebrities' in the context of their own group or community for voicing their opinion online.

A huge informal media has now sprung into existence, written and run by amateur opinion-formers. This informal network of website forums, chat pages, and opinion-editorial columns sits alongside the mainstream media and is hugely influential. In the US, the political website the Drudge Report (**www.drudgereport.com**) has become a political sensation for precisely this reason, as it focuses on US politicians' indiscretions.

3.4   The Drudge Report - www.drudgereport.com

Reputation Case Study: Barack Obama's Presidential Campaign

How you 'manage' this type of informal media is hugely important in protecting your online personal reputation, as demonstrated in this case study about Barack Obama, the 44th US president.

Much of Obama's success has no doubt been due to his charisma, policies, presentation and oratory skills. However, of equal importance during the Presidential elections was his ability to harness the power of the internet and use it to manage his own personal reputation. His ability to do so propelled him to become the US's first black president.

How did he do this? Obama saw that the internet has fostered greater democracy because alongside the mainstream media is a whole new world of professional and amateur websites commenting on every known political issue and cause.

Obama recognised this, and with an unprecedented quantity of donors' money amounting to over $1 billion dollars (44 per cent higher than Clinton[x]), he reached out to individual people online.

3.5 Official presidential portrait of Barack Obama.
Photographed by: Pete Souza, The Obama-Biden Transition Project

3.6 President Obama's Twitter page with number of followers

Under the banner of 'Hope & Change' he unleashed a network of 400 bloggers to personally influence the public discourse and swing voters his way.[xi] This technique was enormously successful and swayed many internet debates, commentaries and opinions in his favour.

In parallel with Kennedy, who was the first president to harness the power of the television, Obama encouraged internet innovations and developments throughout his campaign. When the band Black Eyed Peas posted a video about Obama on the internet, he quickly decided to run it on his homepage.[xii]

In order to foster greater democracy and transparency he even made available his database of supporters on his website.[xiii] This empowered local volunteers to make calls on their own and greatly expanded the number of people working on his campaign.

Whether you're a Democrat or Republican, it's hard not to admire Obama's use of digital technology. His online transparency, creativity and willingness to reach out to as many people as possible made his political campaign irresistible.

If even a President is investing in his online personal reputation, shouldn't you be?

Reputation in the UK political arena

In the UK the business of reputation management is taken very seriously by the main political parties. The conservative party has taken on board a number of reputation management strategies to show their current leader, David Cameron, in a more personal light. Utilising techniques and technologies such as web cams, online polling, YouTube video updates and real-time campaign blogs, the aim is to reach out to the public and assure them that they are being listened to and that the party is being led by a politician who is connected to the people.

The business of politics is a hotbed of reputation, rumour and perception. Being in control of the messages you send and what is being said about you, is crucial in projecting a consistent message and professional profile.

With a general election occurring before the end of 2010, the internet and its ability to disseminate, reflect and spit out good and bad reputation messages, will make this the UK's first online election.

These two-way communication tools are available to everyone – from politicians and business leaders, all the way to school leavers - and they are available to be utilised now.

Celebrity converging at every level

The combination of celebrity mainstream culture, amateur editorial content, voyeurism, and faux celebrity have all occurred in partnership with the growth of the internet.

With speed of information now almost instantaneous and with many websites essentially de facto online publishers, the amount of information being written about people is expanding at an unprecedented rate.

Internet search engines are engaged 24/7 in rapid filtering of information and YOU are now going to have to assume that if you have anything to say or sell it will be exposed and put online.

Be it an opinion, a product, an event, a story or a news item, if it involves you, it will end up online.

Unless you have a comprehensive strategy for managing your personal reputation online, you will be left to the whims and vagaries of other people's opinions.

This is why managing your reputation online is vital – and will become even more so as we move ahead.

KEY LEARNINGS FROM THIS CHAPTER

■ The mainstream media has moved to a populist platform whereby celebrity and the minutiae of people's lives has become a central tenet of their output.

■ This focus on celebrity has infiltrated all levels of society across all media.

■ Celebrity is no longer the preserve of the rich and famous, it also extends to ordinary people – people like you and me – as exemplified by the growth of reality TV.

■ The internet has created a huge rise in the number of groups, networks and communities covering almost every subject and cause imaginable. A huge informal media has sprung into existence, written and run by amateur opinion-formers. Many of these websites are focused on ordinary people, as well as celebrities.

■ This amateur network of website forums, chat pages and opinion-editorial columns sits alongside the mainstream media and is hugely important in the management of your online personal reputation.

■ You must now assume that if you have anything to say or sell it will be exposed and put online.

■ You must have a comprehensive online strategy for protecting your personal reputation in an age when society's focus is on you.

Up next: The law and your reputation

4

The law and your reputation

Protecting yourself

The internet is your reputation battleground. You need to understand and be in control of the remedies available to protect your reputation, and to have a strategy and crisis management plan in place if – or when – there is negative or false content displayed about you. Remember, people find you by searching for you on search engines and in social media spaces. You may be found in business networks, *blogs*, *forums*, *tags* on photographs or videos – in fact, anywhere your name is mentioned on the internet. The *algorithms* that return the search results are agnostic; they don't know if the content that is being returned is saying good or terrible things about you.

You must be aware of this and know what you can do about it.

Many people faced with negative comments will simply say: 'if it's slanderous, I'll get a lawyer on to it.'

With even provincial UK lawyers' fees starting at £150 per hour, this is fine if you can afford it. But even if you can, there is no guarantee that it will solve the problem...

Libel and slander

There are two versions of defamation: libel and slander. Libel is when the defamation is written and slander is when it is verbal. In online law, personal defamation is mainly a libel issue although that is now changing through the use of video postings on sites such as YouTube.

In much of the world, personal defamation has to be proved by the aggrieved party. Therefore, if someone posts something online about you that you feel is wrong, you have to prove that it is incorrect.

More importantly, you have to prove that the libel is damaging to your reputation, career or business.

The judge or jury will then have to confirm that such accusations are false and damaging, and decide on monetary compensation.

It is only individuals who have a prominent public reputation to lose who stand to gain large payouts.

For ordinary people, like you and me, the amount of damages will be negligible, if anything.

Online defamation

In the US, the world benchmark for internet legal jurisdiction, Section 230 of the Communications Decency Act (CDA 230), states that no provider or user of an interactive computer service shall be treated as the publisher or speaker of any information provided by another information content provider.[i]

In plain speak, this grants immunity to website operators if the content is created by a third party.

In even plainer speak, this means that third parties can write what they want about you on a website and pretty much get away with it.

That's not to say people haven't tried to take legal recourse.

One celebrated case in 2006 involved Todd Hollis, a lawyer from Pennsylvania, who actually sued the website mentioned in the last chapter www.dontdatehimgirl.com - for malicious gossip after three women wrote damning reports about his behaviour and conduct. Hollis alleged that the site's proprietor "conspired with disingenuous people whose only agenda was to attack the character of those individuals who have been identified on her site."

The defendant and website owner, Tasha Joseph, counter-argued that, "Suing the site's owner for comments posted on the site was like suing the owner of a coffee shop for the content of private conversations between patrons."

After numerous depositions, the judge dismissed the case citing the lack of personal jurisdiction over Tasha Joseph, in good measure due to Section 230 of the Communications Decency Act.[ii]

In a curious twist, when Hollis filed a second lawsuit, the gloves came off, with Hollis exposing Tasha Joseph as having been convicted of grand theft by the State of Florida. In 2008, after two years, the case was settled out of court with settlement details kept confidential.[iii]

What is important to note is that in the process of seeking legal redress, Hollis made his personal reputation far more public than it would otherwise have been.

Just as importantly, what was a character assassination on one website became truly global as it was replicated on numerous news websites.

For Todd Hollis, repairing his online reputation will be difficult. As for Tasha Joseph, owner of www.dontdatehimgirl.com, the situation is not much better.

Both might have been in a far better position to settle out of court at the start, because while offline reputations fade into memory, online reputations are as fresh as the day they were posted.

Or better still, Hollis should have been aware of the issues and sought to protect his character, by implementing his online reputation strategy across blogs, comments, and his own network to redress the balance.

Criminal records

This leads us to your criminal record.

It's online and it's not going away anytime soon.

Parking fines, speeding tickets, drunk and disorderly – if it's reported in a newspaper, it will be online. Colin Montgomerie, the world famous British golfer, was recently charged with speeding in the London borough of Kingston upon Thames. The news was spread online around the world within minutes.

4.1 Even a world-famous sportsman like Colin Montgomerie had to deal with his criminal activity being plastered all over the internet

For ordinary people the situation is not much different – any conviction will be logged online quickly. Furthermore, it will stay online for years.

While this book is not advocating that you hide any convictions you may have, it will teach you how to manage any negative content and ensure it appears only where you want it to online.

After all, when you meet a person, you don't introduce yourself and say, 'Hi, my name's John and I've just been convicted of a criminal offence.' So why should your online profile be any different?

Reputation Case Study: Lin Jiaxiang

Our fifth case study takes us to China where we can see for ourselves how people's online reputations have gone truly global. It also shows how we are entering an age of trial by internet.

The case in question involves Lin Jiaxiang, a former Communist Party chief and deputy director of the Shenzhen Maritime Safety Administration, who was sacked from his job in November 2008 by China's Ministry of Transport.[iv]

Jiaxiang's offence? Photos and video clips of him surfaced on the internet, which apparently showed him trying to force an 11-year-old girl into the men's toilet of a Shenzhen seafood restaurant, according to the news agency, Reuters.[v]

Chinese online news services subsequently carried interviews with the parents of the 11-year old girl. Allegedly, Jiaxiang had bragged he was a high official from Beijing and offered money to appease them.

4.2   Video clip of footage allegedly showing Lin Jiaxiang taking a young girl to the restrooms to assault her. (Taken from YouTube)

What is interesting about this case, however, is that he was later cleared of child molestation charges.[vi] Xinhua, a major Chinese news organisation also reported that Jiaxiang was "merely drunk and is not a child molester."[vii]

However, thousands of others judged for themselves. For a considerable period, online websites such as **www. reynaelena.com** and YouTube showed the offending video.

Whatever the circumstances of Jiaxiang's sacking, the fact that he was cleared of molestation is almost irrelevant. Thousands saw the video footage and the evidence will be online for years. Indeed, he might be hard pressed to find work again.

This case highlights how in the modern digital age, everyone is able to be judge and jury.

It also shows clearly that people's online reputations span international boundaries.

Your online profile is now worldwide.

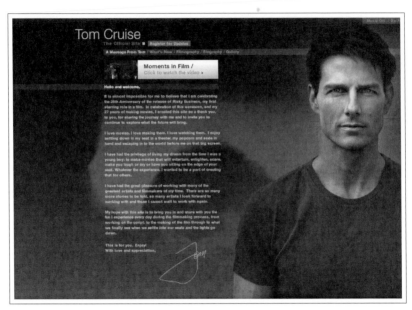

4.3   The official Tom Cruise website – www.tomcruise.com

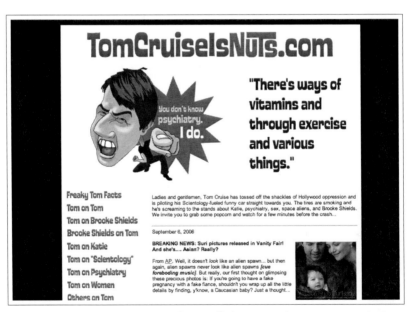

4.4   One of many unofficial Tom Cruise websites – www.tomcruiseisnuts.com

Data protection

A word about data protection: it won't help you.

Most western governments record all emails, web searches and website visits. While this data is held securely, there is no guarantee that it won't ever be leaked or accidentally made public.

In fact, the majority of data security breaches are via government departments and it is estimated that 60 million people worldwide have had data about themselves exposed.[viii]

In Europe, data protection is governed by the EU Directive 95/46/EC 1995 on the Protection of Individuals. However, while this means that private information held on you by commercial organisations and Government departments is legally meant to be secure, the various legislation directives cannot guarantee that data security accidents won't occur.

More importantly, data protection cannot prevent other people from posting information on you or making it available on the web.

By way of example, type 'Tom Cruise' into Google's search engine. The Hollywood actor's own official website, **www.tomcruise.com**, scores highly but so do his YouTube videos about Scientology, as well as the antagonistic 'TomCruiseIsNuts' website. No amount of data protection legislation can stop this material registering on Tom Cruise's first search engine results page.

And if Tom Cruise isn't in control of what is written about him, you can be assured that neither are you.

But don't panic. While you can't control what other people write about you online, you can develop strategies to manage how it appears online and what you can do to put yourself in the best light possible.

ID fraud

Identity fraud (ID fraud) is the fraudulent use of confidential or personal information that has been stolen. Fraudsters will use this data for many purposes including setting up credit cards, bank accounts or credit with suppliers using your business or personal details.

In 2007, 3.58 per cent of US adults were victims of identity fraud[ix] while the British Security Industry Association estimates it costs the UK economy £1.7 billion a year.[x]

One company recently conducted an experiment during which they placed a job advertisement in a national paper for a bogus company called Denis Atlas (an anagram of 'steal an ID') and launched a site for people to send their CVs to. By the end of the week, this so-called 'employer' had received 107 CVs containing personal information about candidates.[xi]

Criminals typically only need three out of 15 key pieces of information to steal your identity.

Worse still, ID fraud can have implications for your online personal reputation.

You need to know how to minimise the damage to your online personal reputation if someone steals your identity and misrepresents you online.

Remember, your personal reputation is everything.

- It is your personal currency;

- It is your identity;

- It is your own personal 'brand';

- **Protect it.**

KEY LEARNINGS FROM THIS CHAPTER:

■ In online law, personal defamation is mainly a libel issue, although that is now changing through the use of video postings on sites such as YouTube.

■ To be legally successful, you have to prove that the libel is damaging to your reputation and career. It is, therefore, only individuals who have a prominent public reputation who stand to gain large payouts.

■ For ordinary people, legal redress is not an option because of the costs involved and the lack of recompense even if they win the case.

■ In the US, the leading world authority for internet legal jurisdiction, Section 230 of the Communications Decency Act (CDA 230), says that third parties can write what they want about you on a website and pretty much get away with it.

■ Negative content about you can stick around for years.

■ Data protection legislation cannot prevent other people posting information about you and making it available on the web.

■ In 2007, 3.58 per cent of US adults were victims of identity fraud and this figure is set to grow. Much of this ID fraud involves online transactions.

■ Given the lack of legal redress it is crucial that you protect your own online reputation using the techniques we will discuss in the second part of this book.

Up next: Social media

5

Social media

What is social media?

Social media is a collection of websites or networks that enable people to interact and collaborate together online.

Anybody who has ever ventured online has probably used social media at one time or other: typical examples include Google Groups (reference, *social networking*), Wikipedia (reference), MySpace (social networking), Facebook (social networking), Youmeo (social network aggregation), Last.fm (music sharing), YouTube (social networking and video sharing), Second Life (*virtual reality*), Flickr (photo sharing), Twitter (social networking and *microblogging*), Skype (internet phonecalls) and Digg (*social bookmarking*).

The key word is 'share' and social media allows you to share information with chosen friends and contacts far more efficiently than simply emailing or texting everyone separately.

Just as importantly, while industrial media such as TV and newspapers require heavy investment, social media tools are cheap – usually free of charge – and available to all on a global basis.

It's this 'free of charge' aspect, just like email, that has helped turn social media into a global phenomenon. The ability to connect, engage and interact with like-minded people easily and quickly is the key differentiator from old style one-way communication.

5.1 Leading social media brands and tools

How big is social media?

To put this market into context, 63 per cent of all UK internet users visit a social media website each month – representing 21 per cent year-on-year growth.[i]

In the US, the picture is broadly similar with social media now accounting for more than five of the top ten biggest internet sites.[ii] MySpace, for example, is now the third biggest website in the US with 72 million unique monthly visitors[iii] after Google and Yahoo!.

Social media – an educated audience

Social media users are generally well educated. YouTube reaches over 62 million US people between 18 and 24, have a household income of over $60,000 (£38,000), and of which 53 per cent have attended college or graduate school.[iv]

But how does social media affect me?

With an infinite network of possible channels available to spread your message, all the rules of engagement have changed. Your life can be lived out online in any number of ways; your online profiles can cover multiple personalities, types, ages, and opinions. Now you never have to be the real you at all, but this is missing the point. What's important is that you realise your views, interests and status are available 24/7.

Many thousands of your peers and colleagues don't recognise this – or don't even have a presence online. For the reputation savvy, this is a real opportunity to promote and enhance your prospects. What better way to show your audience how professional and effective you are by putting out a consistent message across the areas they are most likely to look for you?

Social media networks are organised around people, with the individual at the centre of their own community.

Put simply, you are now the celebrity of your *online community*.

WHICH SOCIAL MEDIA SITES ARE YOUR TARGET AUDIENCE USING?

▶ Where are they likely to look for you?

▶ Is it business social media sites such as LinkedIn?

▶ Microblogging platforms like Twitter?

▶ More informal social media spaces like MySpace or Bebo?

▶ Think about which sites reflect your personal brand and which you would be happy to be associated with.

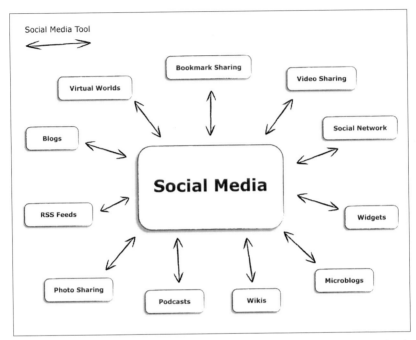

Social Media Tool

Virtual Worlds

Bookmark Sharing

Video Sharing

Blogs

Social Network

Social Media

RSS Feeds

Widgets

Photo Sharing

Podcasts

Wikis

Microblogs

5.2 There are several elements that make up social media

Being a celebrity of your own community has its benefits, of course – 'public displays of connection' serve as important identity markers that help people feel comfortable in the networked social world, and a large network can validate your personal identity.

Social media also allows a person to present an idealised version of themselves online – whether it's accurate or fantasised (as in virtual worlds such as Second Life (**www.secondlife.com**) where individuals create idealised avatars of how they would like to be perceived; these can be reflections of their real-world selves or as outrageous as the imagination will allow). This gives people a greater freedom than they often feel they have in the offline world.

Such is the power of social media over individuals that they have become deeply embedded in user's lives. In Korea, the social media website Cyworld (**us.cyworld.com**) has become an integral part of everyday life with 85 per cent of people listing 'the maintenance and reinforcement of pre-existing social networks as their main motive for Cyworld use.'[v]

Dark side of the moon

However, while social media has been a hugely positive development, like most innovations, there is a potential dark side to it.

Yes, it allows people to share information about themselves and their friends quickly, efficiently and semi-publicly.

But it also makes deeply personal information suddenly available online for others to see.

The management of your social media profile(s) is, therefore, crucial to your ability to manage your online personal reputation.

You've been YouTubed

Alongside Facebook, perhaps the biggest social media phenomenon has been video-sharing website YouTube. The company was only founded in February 2005 but its enormous growth helped persuade Google to buy it 18 months later for $1.65 billion. The website is currently ranked as the third biggest in the world[vi].

Indeed, the fastest growing segment of the UK social media sector is video-sharing websites such as YouTube.

Worldwide, over 10 billion videos were watched online in December 2007 alone.[vii]

The question is, were you on one of them?

If so, does it reflect the personal reputation you want to project or is it something you'd prefer was not publicly available?

Remember, unless you have an existing commercial agreement with the person taking the video, you have no copyright control over any footage taken of you. In addition, once it's put online by another person it can be difficult to remove it yourself.

Therefore, it is vital you learn how to manage any video content featuring you that is posted online.

A shift in the organisation of communities

Social media represents a major shift in the organisation of communities.

The world is now composed of networks and this means your personal information travels well beyond your immediate sphere of influence or group.

While you are in charge of your own individual community, you are not in charge of others' communities. You are, therefore, not in control of what other people think, write or say about you.

Suddenly you are exposed: videos on YouTube, photos on Flickr, comments on Facebook and so on. All these represent a threat to you because other people are now able to affect your reputation online without your permission.

To get the true value of social media, it's vital you are able to manage what is written and put online about you so it serves your best interests.

Do it well and you are already halfway towards protecting and enhancing your online personal reputation.

We will show you how to do this (and more) in the following chapters and fully equip you with all the knowledge and techniques you'll need.

KEY LEARNINGS FROM THIS CHAPTER:

- Social media is an internet phenomenon and 63 per cent of all UK internet users visit a social media website each month.

- Social media users are, in the main, an educated audience.

- The fastest growing segment of the UK social media sector is video-sharing websites, such as YouTube.

- Social media allows you to share information with chosen friends and contacts far more efficiently than simply emailing or texting each person separately. It has accelerated the dissemination of information faster than ever before.

- Social media represents a major shift in the organisation of communities. The world is now composed of networks and this means your personal information travels beyond your immediate sphere of influence.

- Social media networks are organised around people, not interests, with the individual at the centre of their own community. You are now the celebrity of your online community.

- While you are in charge of your own individual community, you are not in charge of others' communities. You are, therefore, not in control of what other people write or say about you.

- Social media makes deeply personal information suddenly available online for others to see. The effective management of your social media profile(s) is crucial to the success of your online personal reputation.

Read on to the next chapter: Defining yourself online

6

Defining yourself online

In this chapter, you will:

- Begin developing your reputation strategy
- Understand your target audience and what they are looking for
- Learn what your current online profile looks like
- Define your 'brand values' (what you stand for)
- Start creating your online framework and profile
- Group the information about yourself that people will be searching for (achievements, background, status and interests) into a logical structure

What you know already

Your personal reputation is of the utmost importance – and that's true of your reputation offline in the real world or online in the virtual world.

Yet until now, most people haven't paid much attention to their reputation online. A misguided belief still lingers in the public mindset that if you're not posting anything about yourself online – be that a blog, holiday snaps, or feedback on eBay, for example – then you're essentially not online.

But to take such a view is wrong, naïve even.

What other people say and upload about you online is open to the rest of the world, whether you like it or not. You can't ever really 'control' the internet;

other people can influence your reputation and the perception people have of you through the comments they make on your profile page on Facebook, the pictures that friends upload of you on Flickr and so on.

What you do on the internet also has a huge influence on your personal reputation online: the forums you join, the comments you post on social network sites, the clubs you belong to... All of this makes up the image of 'you' that exists online – and it is available to your employer, potential employer, business contact or anyone using a search engine to find out about you.

Given how much time, energy and money we invest in protecting and promoting ourselves offline – through the clothes we wear, the car we drive or the reputation we carve out for ourselves at work – shouldn't we be thinking about how people perceive us online too?

We've told you why it's important to manage your personal reputation in the previous chapters. In this chapter, we're going to tell you how to begin taking control of it.

▲▲ Search engines continue to be the primary tool people use to navigate the Web ▼▼

Jason Levin, analyst at Nielsen/NetRatings

The bad news...

Life online may move at a faster pace than it does offline – news stories are updated by the minute, Twitter feeds track events as they happen – but some things occur at the same pace whether they're in the real or the virtual world.

So just as in the offline world, where you have to cultivate friendships, nurture business connections and establish trust with colleagues, it takes time to build up a reputation for yourself online.

That's not just down to human nature and our desire to 'connect' with others, but due to technology too.

The usual starting point for users online is Google. In October 2008, an estimated 4.8 billion search queries in the US were conducted on Google Search, representing 61.2 per cent of all search queries conducted that month.[i] In the UK, it's a similar story: Google Search was the most popular website in 2007, averaging 25.1 million British visitors each month.[ii]

So why does this matter? Because search engines, social media searches and blog searches are where people will look for you. It makes good reputation sense to ensure that the content they find is based on your professional profile along with those elements of your personal profile that you want to project - ensuring you take advantage of the technology available to communicate your message clearly and effectively.

REPUTATION NOTE

* Getting search engines to notice you online does take time.

... The good news

The time issue can be overcome. Internet marketers and online advertisers know that they can promote their new product or service on the web quickly and cost effectively, so why shouldn't you be able to do the same?

It doesn't have to take months to begin managing your personal reputation online. If you understand the basic principles and how to apply some simple techniques, you can raise your profile online quickly and efficiently.

Back to basics

Protecting your online personal reputation isn't rocket science. You don't have to be an internet geek or technology whizz kid to get yourself noticed online.

In fact, as with most things in life, getting the basics right will build a foundation for the future.

What we are talking about is developing your online reputation strategy.

Having a definable online reputation strategy means you understand how important your reputation is to your professional success and you are committed to improving it. By understanding your strengths and weaknesses, building a consistent online profile, and knowing your target audience, you can begin to sketch out a reputation plan of action.

Once your reputation profile is consistent across all of your online outlets and you are actively managing and monitoring your reputation through online tools, you will be way ahead of the curve.

Simple. So where do we begin?

Step 1: Your primary aim

First things first: you need to decide what your aim is in managing your reputation online.

Are you a graduate looking for your first break? Are you a company director looking to communicate better with your customers? Or perhaps you're worried about job security, and looking for a head start should the worst happen.

You might be looking to promote yourself to potential employers, win new business or a pay rise, or protect your reputation from competitors. Through personal reputation management, you can take care of all these possible scenarios and more.

The fact of the matter is that personal reputation is crucial, whether you're starting your career or have a wealth of experience behind you.

The internet might not be a 'controllable' medium, but you can certainly put in place some steps to protect – as well as promote – yourself online.

REPUTATION ACTION: YOUR PRIMARY OBJECTIVES

✔ Write down your primary aim for managing your reputation online (i.e. get a job, secure a promotion or protect your reputation from competitors).

✔ Who is your intended audience (An employer, headhunter or new customer)?

✔ Where would your audience expect to find you (Facebook, Twitter, your website or blog)?

The internet is your route to future opportunities

Remember, the internet isn't just a great place to find out what your friends are doing, check the football scores or download the latest music from iTunes. It's a place where you can find out about potential job opportunities, locate new business contacts and crucially, get yourself noticed by your intended audience.

The key question is, will what people find out about you online be what you want them to see?

The bigger picture over the next few years

For many people, fear of losing their jobs will be justifiably uppermost in their thoughts at present. Unemployment has already risen to around six per cent, with the number of people out of work in the UK increasing to 2.38 million in the second quarter of 2009.[iii] The forecast looks equally grim, with one professional body, the Chartered Institute of Personnel and Development, predicting the loss of an additional 600,000 jobs in the UK in 2009.[iv]

For everyone in the labour market – whether graduates or school leavers trying to get their first jobs, to people already in employment or recently made redundant – these are difficult times, and few economists are daring to predict the situation will get better in the short term.

But rather than despair, consider what you can do to promote yourself and get ahead in the current climate. Personal reputation management is relevant not just when you're looking for your next job but at any point during your career. Remember, some employers are still recruiting – even in a downturn – and if you can't be found online, it will be nigh on impossible for them to consider you for a job inthe first place.

If you're a recent graduate, there's no denying that the number of jobs available has shrunk since the recession began. But this is the perfect time to take

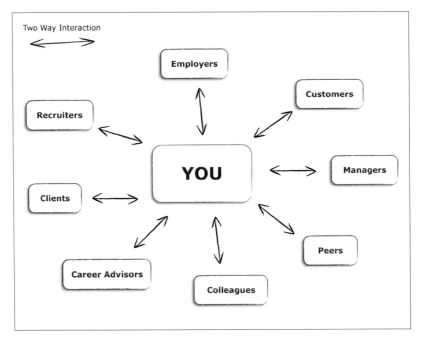

6.1 Your Stakeholders

advantage of the current situation and use it as an opportunity to promote yourself above your peers and take control of your personal reputation.

Think about it: if you were an employer with 50 CVs on your desk, where would you go to find out more about the candidates? Sure you'll want to make a shortlist of the best candidates and interview them formally face to face or over the telephone, but you'll probably take a look online first to see if you can find out any more about them, wouldn't you?

Step 2: Your online profile audit

REPUTATION ACTION: AUDIT YOUR CURRENT REPUTATION ONLINE

✔ Take a moment to think about how your current online profile looks.

WHERE ARE YOU LISTED?

✔ Refer back to the Reputation Action from chapter 1 (page 20) in which you noted those websites that you interacted with the most.

✔ Review these websites along with any others where you know you are listed or referenced – such as your blogs, personal websites, company pages, or social networks such as Twitter, Flickr, Facebook and MySpace. Now consider which of the content on these sites you wouldn't want a prospective employer or business contact to see. This is your first step towards cleaning up your online profile.

REPUTATION ACTION: AUDIT YOUR CURRENT REPUTATION ONLINE (CONT.)

THE IMPORTANCE OF SEARCH IN DEFINING YOURSELF ONLINE

- ✔ Now think about your target audience: employers with too little time to review all the candidates for their job or customers who want the most hassle-free buying option.

- ✔ But don't forget about your other key audience; the one that deals in facts and statistics and to which you can't appeal to on an emotional level: the major search engines.

- ✔ Type your name into Google, Yahoo! and one other search engine. Do you appear in the first three pages of any of the results? If not, try narrowing your search down to country-specific sites only, depending on where you're based.

- ✔ The chances are you're already online in some capacity – perhaps you have a Facebook or Bebo profile page, maybe you've been in the local paper which is archived online, or maybe you're a member of a football group with an online forum. If you've been in employment for a long time, there's also a chance your name might be connected to your current or previous jobs, perhaps.

- ✔ If there's nothing online about you, your audience won't be able to find you.

- ✔ But if you do appear in the search engine listings, use the list of categories below to note all of the online places where you are mentioned. Maybe these are sites you have a profile on, blogs that you have commented on or sites where others are posting content about you:

  - ■ Websites

- Blog sites

- Social network / social media sites

- Your own website

- Your own blog

- Contributing / commenting blogs

- Your company website

- Your friends' websites

✔ Now look at these sites in more detail. Consider what they say about you. For a start, what's publicly available for anyone to see? What kind of person do the results suggest you are? What do they indicate your skills are or where your interests lie?

✔ Have you found any references to yourself that you didn't expect to see? Be honest with yourself – does this newly found online content that you or others have posted about you reflect you as the professional, creative, dedicated person that you wish to be perceived as? Does it make you look employable? Trustworthy? Someone you'd want to do business with?

✔ Most importantly, are you seeing the image of yourself that you want to portray?

Now you know who your intended audience is and your current online status, so you can begin putting it all together into an online framework. This is the simple process of understanding how best to promote yourself and your reputation online.

Who do you think is going to impress an employer most? A candidate whose website appears in the first page of Google's *search rankings*, alongside other results to their LinkedIn profile and perhaps an article written in their student newspaper? Or a candidate whose search results reveal some compromising photos on Flickr of a drunken graduation party and an open Facebook profile with highlights of the candidate's debauched holiday to Ibiza written about on his wall? It's no contest, is it?

The same applies to professionals, company directors and business owners. Whoever your intended audience is, it is up to you to ensure that they can find you online and that what they find presents you in the best light possible.

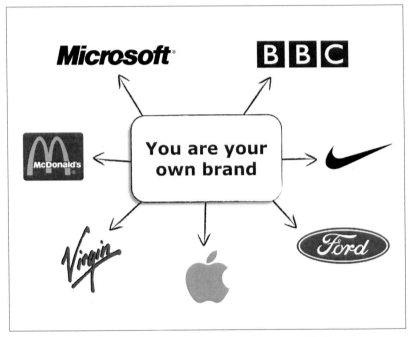

6.2 You are your own brand

You are a brand

What is a good brand? A good brand improves or enhances your life in some way. Whether a fashion or international travel brand, good brands utilise the same techniques to identify themselves and their *offering*, often in a crowded market place. They can be helpful, useful, stylish or utilitarian; whatever the brand offers, if it is successful it will be carefully planned and managed.

You can do the same with your reputation, and use the same branding techniques to enhance your profile. If you think about how brands are perceived, there is often a unique proposition (in this case that is you); they fulfil a need (there is a job vacancy that needs filling, an offering or service that a customer requires); and when you mention your professional life (your key knowledge or experience), you talk about yourself and your offering consistently (marketing yourself).

Put all these elements together and your professional profile becomes clearer and easier to understand – exactly how a well-executed brand would work.

Step 3: Creating your online framework

The best way to think about your online framework is as a set of 'pillars' that cover how you will present, structure and group together all the professional and personal information about yourself that you want people to find when they search for you online.

Your online framework encompasses more than just information about yourself; it's also about how you convey your personality. For example, the keywords or taglines you use in signatures or blogs, or maybe the colours or fonts you use online to reflect your personality. It might be your language style when you comment on blogs, or the style in which you have designed your personal website (eg. colourful, formal, minimalist, retro, hard-edged....) Together, these 'pillars' describe who you are online.

Q. WHAT IF I DONT WANT TO LOSE THE PERSONAL REPUTATION I ALREADY HAVE ONLINE?

- You'll probably have found when you searched for yourself online that the search engine results contained a mixture of personal and professional web links. A mixture of those you've created and those others have created about you. It's ok to have a social life online, in fact, the internet is the main form of communication for many under-30-year-olds.

- Facebook experienced its biggest spike in traffic ever in the UK on Christmas Day 2008, which on its own is testimony to the importance of many people's virtual lives.[v]

- But what you do need to think about is how you separate out your personal and professional lives online, and the protection you put in place around the 'personal' you so it's not visible to those that you want to find out about you online in a professional capacity.

Before you work out in detail how you want to present yourself online and how to incorporate your key 'pillars', you first need to decide exactly what you want to say about yourself online and how you are going to describe yourself.

Knowing your *'brand values'* will help you to build up a framework of what you want people to think about you when they search for you online. It's the thought process marketers go through when preparing for a new product launch.

REPUTATION ACTION: WORK OUT WHO YOU ARE – YOUR BRAND VALUES

✔ Try some of the classic branding exercises marketers use when working on a new product launch. This time though, remember the product is You. Take some time to write down your answers to the following questions:

1. What brands are you aligned with personally, which reflect the key elements of you and your professional profile and why?

2. Which brands would you dislike being associated with? (What are the worst brands you could think of and why?)

3. Who are the professional people you connect with or aspire to be like and why?

4. What words would you use to describe yourself and what you have to offer professionally?

5. What words would others use to describe you? (Ask colleagues or friends for a fair appraisal - honesty is the best policy when you are defining your own brand.)

6. If you were a car, film, country, actor or animal, which type would it be?

7. What are your key brand characteristics (fun, energy, credibility, dedication)?

Looking and feeling the part - your online profile

If you were going for a job interview or meeting a client or customer for the first time, you'd take time to consider what you looked like and whether you had everything with you that you needed to fulfil the task. Essentially you'd do everything to make sure you looked and felt the part.

Putting your online profile together involves exactly the same thought process. The only difference is that the environment in which you're presenting yourself is now the internet, which means you need to think about the information you want to project about yourself online, and how you want to project that information, as this is what people will use to construct a picture of you.

If you're looking for the next step up the career ladder, or to gain attention for your company or business, you want whatever's written about you online to position you positively. It's the online equivalent of dressing for the job you want or demonstrating the skills that the promotion requires.

One of the biggest changes this requires is a shift in mindset from not thinking about your reputation as the cornerstone of your brand, to understanding how powerful your brand as an individual can be.

It might sound like marketing gobbledygook but thinking about yourself as a brand helps separate out the professional 'you' from the personal 'you'.

Now it's time to start putting some substance behind your online framework.

The World Wide Web presents... You

By this point, you should have decided what your aim is in managing your personal reputation online and given some thought to how you want to be portrayed after investigating your current online profile.

Now it's time to start promoting 'you' to potential employers, business contacts and customers.

If you think about how you promote yourself in the offline world, you probably use techniques such as describing what stage you're at now, your achievements to date, perhaps your educational background and a bit about your personal interests and passions – this applies whether you are talking to prospective employers, recruitment agencies, headhunters or business contacts.

You will want your online profile to outline key parts of the professional 'you', even if the environment in which it's displayed is different.

The first step is to begin cleaning up your profile.

REPUTATION ACTION: CREATING AN EXECUTIVE SUMMARY

✔ Now that you've completed your audit, and have listed out the sites, blogs and networks where content about you is being displayed, you can begin the process of cleaning up, repairing or just enhancing your online profile.

✔ This step involves identifying the few key things that you would want people to find out about you.

✔ If a prospective employer or business contact were to ask you what your key strengths are, what would you say? List your top five strengths.

✔ Now think about your aspirations. What kind of business or role would be your ideal fit? Maybe this is something that plays on your key strengths, or maybe it is a new area of expertise that you would like to move into.

EXECUTIVE SUMMARY OF YOU

✔ Now you can begin to start formulating your executive summary – this is a brief description of yourself that highlights your key strengths and your aspirations. It will help outline what you can bring to an employer, a business partner or even what type of service you could offer a new customer. This will also relate your strengths to your desires; essentially what you are looking for in your ideal situation.

✔ This can be quite a difficult exercise, and you won't get it right first time, but have a go now. You will come back to your executive summary in a later chapter and can continue to refine it as you learn more about creating your online reputation.

Digital 'touchpoints'

It is worth remembering that your online framework elements can be utilised across all of your digital touchpoints, whether they are your blog, your own website, your company website, any of the social media networks, and even your emails.

The key though, is to convey a consistent message across all touchpoints so that whether a person is searching for you on Twitter, through blog posts or comments, or is looking through their archived emails for potential job candidates, they understand quickly what you stand for and what skills, experience or service you can offer them.

Think about the consistency of the story you are telling through your online framework. Use key phrases and words to show you in your best light and to help clarify the best aspects of your brand.

Building blocks

Bearing in mind how people read and digest information online – and how you can re-use what you write across multiple channels – you should keep any content you write about yourself concise and to the point. A 500-word post on your blog about your professional background is fine, but you should also be able to convey key information that an employer might want to know about you in 50 words or less. Even more importantly, the information a search engine will return when someone searches for you will be around 20 words in length. So remember to keep it simple, clear and direct.

6.3   A personal website can be an important component of your online profile

The executive summary – your succinct calling card

Write three executive summaries of 15, 50 and 200 words each to deal with most online situations (email signature, blog comment signature, initial job enquiry and so on). Once written these words form a powerful toolbox of content that can be used across a variety of digital communications, providing you with a simple but effective hub of key summaries that let your audience know who you are and what you are all about.

Once you've developed your summary you can move onto your 'big four' professional statements. These are four self-explanatory headings (achievements, status, background, interests) with no more than 250 words under each. These headings can be utilised in any number of instances online.

The 'big four' pillars of your professional statement – and where to apply them

This is where you start to flesh out the image you want to project about yourself online. Refer back to your aims and objectives: what is your primary motivating force? A new job? Career enhancement? New business opportunities? Think about who you are targeting and why.

Your complete online profile should present all of the best bits about you – succinctly written – and can be conveyed through your 'big four' professional statements. So whether you are writing content for your blog, your website, your company website, or any of the social media networks you belong to, you can refer back to your professional statements at all times to see which words, phrases, information or content fit best. Little things like understanding where your strengths are and letting everyone know what you're good at are incredibly powerful tools to have at your disposal.

Your own website or blog should contain lots of relevant information or posts about your interest areas, passions, points of difference and *unique selling points (USPs)*, as well as your professional statements.

So what are your 'big four' professional statements?

The main things people will be looking for when they look you up online are:

* Your achievements;

* Your status;

* Your background;

* Your interests.

Let's look at each one now in more detail.

1. Your achievements

Your achievements can be anything that you think demonstrate your talents, skills and knowledge. It might be the launch of a new business or product line, a quick promotion at work, or recognition from your industry through a prize or reward.

But achievements don't just have to be related to the world of work – if you're a student starting out in employment, you probably won't have many work-related achievements to list anyway – but you can also refer to educational achievements, perhaps some fundraising you've done for charity, or maybe you've achieved something through your hobbies or interests that you're particularly proud of.

What's important is that you can explain why you consider it to be an achievement and how it's helped your professional development.

REPUTATION ACTION: YOUR ACHIEVEMENTS

✔ List as many achievements as you can think of in five minutes. Don't worry about the level of detail at this stage; just write as many achievements down as possible, in the time allocated. Think broadly across your different jobs, businesses, hobbies, training and learning.

REPUTATION ACTION: YOUR ACHIEVEMENTS (CONT.)

✔ You might also want to take time to ask people who know you – such as friends, family, fellow students perhaps, or colleagues – to find out what they think have been your biggest achievements. You might be surprised at their response or it might remind you of something you'd achieved but since forgotten.

✔ Now whittle down your long list to a shortlist of your five best achievements and include an explanatory sentence or two (no more than a short paragraph) for each one to explain why you think it's an achievement and what opportunities it gave you.

---

2. Your status

When we meet someone for the first time, the initial five minutes are usually spent identifying what stage each person is at in their life in order to find some common ground or interests. Online, it's no different. This is why we suggest including a section on your status so people searching for you will know in an instant what stage you're at in your life and what you're doing currently.

REPUTATION ACTION: YOUR STATUS

✔ Write down a straightforward description of where you're at now: are you employed? Recently graduated? Looking for new opportunities? Establishing a new business partnership?

✔ Don't include any information on your age, as recent discrimination legislation in the UK prevents employers

REPUTATION ACTION: YOUR STATUS (CONT.)

from taking age into consideration when selecting the best candidate to fill a post.

✔ Also make sure you don't include too much personal information, such as your address or date of birth. This isn't only for legal reasons, but to avoid identity fraud.

3. Your background

To understand where you are now, people need to know a bit about your background and how you've reached your current position. Even if you're a school leaver, it's important to give some historical detail to your working life so far.

REPUTATION ACTION: YOUR BACKGROUND

✔ Write down a brief history of your professional life. If you've been working, write a short history of what industries you've worked in, what skills you've developed, where you've been employed and what your current area of expertise is. You'll perhaps want to briefly note your educational achievements too, where relevant.

✔ Even if you've just graduated or left school, you still have a background, so write down where you were educated and any grades or educational recognition you achieved in that time.

4. Your interests

This is often the forgotten bit on people's CVs, but don't underestimate the importance of your interests or hobbies in giving potential employers, business contacts or customers an insight into your personality.

The chief executive of one advertising agency told us that a person's interests are what he uses to decide whether to employ someone. "If a CV has reached me, it's already been read by lots of people and everyone is telling me that this is an appropriate person for the vacancy. So then the question becomes how does each candidate differentiate him or herself? I only want to work with interesting people so I look at their interests to find out whether they're a boring or an interesting person."

So don't leave out your interests because you think they're of little relevance to prospective employers, customers or recruiters. People want to find out about you – give them the information they're looking for.

REPUTATION ACTION: YOUR INTERESTS

✔ Write a list of between three and five interests. Try to come up with a variety to demonstrate a well-rounded personality.

✔ Don't panic: this doesn't mean that you have to have an Olympic gold medal in swimming or dedicate all your spare time to aid work in Africa. But it does mean thinking about what the interests you have say about you and perhaps re-phrasing the way you describe your hobbies. 'I'm an expert on The Sopranos' sounds far more captivating than 'I like watching TV', for example.

Every time you say goodbye

There is one important piece of your online framework that we mustn't forget. Each and every blog post, comment, email or reply that you make should be signed off with a status update about you.

Think of your sign-off or signature as an opportunity to let people know your current status – and to let them know you are available for meetings, job offers or business opportunities. Your sign-offs are also another opportunity to promote the other elements of your online profile.

For example:

> *Best regards,*
> *John Smith*
>
> *PS. I'm available for web design work from June 1st. View my portfolio at www.johnsmithdesigner.com. Call me on 07748 948 899 for more details.*

It's all about consistency of the message

Everything we've talked about so far involves establishing, enhancing or cleaning up your digital profile. It's about separating out the professional and personal 'you' online and, ultimately, helping you put your best foot forward in your professional life.

KEY LEARNINGS FROM THIS CHAPTER

■ Your reputation strategy begins with defining your primary objectives first. Are you looking for a new job? Career enhancement? Or a new business opportunity?

■ You must know who your target audience is and be visible on the sites they use (search engines, blogs, social networks and so on).

■ Conducting an online audit will focus you on the current state of your online reputation and form the basis of what actions you need to take next.

■ Your online framework consists of your executive summary, achievements, status, background and interests (the 'big four' pillars). It is a great way to organise the elements of 'you' that your audience needs to know about in a professional capacity.

■ Writing an executive summary helps to focus on your key strengths and to define what opportunities you are looking for.

■ Your framework elements form the cornerstone of your brand.

■ Your online CV is not like a traditional, linear, paper-based CV. It is anywhere that information about you can be found online – from blogs to social networks, your own or your company's website.

■ Writing long and short versions of your online framework makes it easy to distribute your profile information across multiple websites, blogs, comments, email communication or social media networks and helps to deliver your key messages effectively.

■ Be consistent in the message you convey; your reputation is now a valuable asset and you need to protect it.

- Make sure your 'brand values' are consistent across your executive summary and your 'big four' professional statements, and that they tally up with your personality. You're the brand in this context and although you're seeking to manage your personal reputation online, you don't want to appear as someone you're not.

- The online and offline worlds are merging. The management of your online personal reputation, therefore, has many ramifications across every aspect of your life.

- It is up to you to define how you are seen online.

What's next for your online framework?

So by this point you should understand your primary aims, have defined your 'brand values' (what you stand for), understand the importance of creating an online framework, and know what kinds of information people will be searching for on you: your achievements, your background, your status and your interests.

In the next chapter, we'll explore what you can do with your online framework to start promoting your personal reputation online. We'll also examine the different technologies available to use when promoting yourself and how you can build your own website to focus exclusively on you.

Read on to the next chapter: Tools & technology

7

Tools & technology

In this chapter, you will:

- Find out about the online tools you can use to develop or enhance your online reputation
- Choose which social media networks are best for your particular circumstance
- Use simple non-technical tools to create your own webspace or blog
- Get to grips with domain names and hosting
- Utilise your online framework content to create a consistent profile

All about you

If you've got this far, you already know personal reputation management is crucial to developing a successful career or business. You'll also have started to think about what you want people to find out about you online and how to use the internet to create an online framework that shows you and 'your brand' in the best possible light.

In this chapter, we'll look at the tools that already exist online to help you cultivate and protect your reputation online. We'll also advise you on using social media spaces to ensure you create a consistent and professional profile. Finally, we'll show you how to create a website – your own space – that you can use to create a hub for your online presence, and use your online framework to show what you are all about.

Where to promote your reputation on the internet

At this point you know that there are multiple channels on the internet from which you can promote your personal reputation. By following the steps outlined in chapter 6 in setting out your online profile framework and 'big four' pillars, you are now in a great position to begin filling in the gaps in the management of your reputation across your own website, your company website, blogs and social networks.

However, although spreading your message to the maximum amount of people is a key factor, you must avoid the scattergun approach. You do not have to fill each social media site available on the internet with every conceivable piece of information about you, as managing and updating all of these is time consuming and ineffective.

It is a sensible step to have one or two 'central hubs' - typically your own website or blog - where your key content will sit and where prospective employers or customers can find out more detail about you and what you have to offer. Then the trick is to utilise the relevant social media spaces – such as LinkedIn, Facebook or Twitter – for punchy, relevant and timely communication to your audience. For instance, in the case of Twitter this could be real-time updates on your status and availability, whereas your blog might be used to push across different strands of your interests and ideas. Remember, your short executive summary is perfect for signing off on blog posts, as a footnote to any articles you might write online or as your digital calling card in all your professional communications.

Having your main messages on your own website can take a little longer to set up but the results are worth it. For instance, it can often be easier to get the search engines to *index (See Site indexing)* a personal website or blog than it is to index all of your multiple social media profiles.

The end result of utilising all these different channels for your message, is that when a recruiter or a customer searches for information about you on a search engine they will find a wide range of information. Ideally this will include your own website or blog, two professional profiles, perhaps an article you've written and one or two of your social media spaces. 'Owning' the first page of Google is a great credibility indicator and helps your audience understand what you have to offer. It also has the added benefit of relegating existing negative or unprofessional content about you further down the search engine results.

The technology already exists

If you look around on the web, there are hundreds, if not thousands, of websites where you can create your own content. Best of all, most of these are free and easily available for you to use and start managing your online reputation.

In fact, the chances are you're using some of these websites and social media sites already: your own website, your company website, Blogger, Wordpress, Facebook, MySpace, YouTube, Flickr, Twitter. You name it, you've probably already heard of some of these websites, joined or had access to at least one of these sites to connect with colleagues, customers or friends, upload photos or videos, and interact with other people from all over the internet.

These are powerful tools that you can use to promote you and your brand online. And you can do it simply and quickly to maximise your personal reputation, giving you a fighting chance of landing that new job or lucrative piece of new business.

Don't worry, it won't be too painful an exercise

You don't necessarily have to develop your own website, post thousands of blog entries or trawl through hundreds of social media sites to extend the reach of your online reputation. You just have to be consistent with your messages, pick the right tools for you and avoid information overload.

Choosing the right social media tools for you

There are a huge variety of social media sites to choose from, some of which you or your company may already have a profile on or have already used to post a blog or comment. They all appear similar but have some major differences in who would view them and why – differences that will affect whether they are the right choice for your personal circumstances.

If you are new to the internet and social media, try a selection of them first to get a feel for whether you think that prospective employers or contacts would be likely to use them and whether you would be likely to use them in a professional capacity.

Remember, if you already have one or several social media profiles the key is to get rid of unprofessional content by separating out the personal 'you' from the professional 'you': reviewing all images and links, and ensuring what your target audience finds when they search for you online is consistent and professional.

We don't recommend setting up multiple social media profiles or blogs just because it is possible. It is much better to focus on the two or three that are relevant to you and the management of your individual reputation. This might to be to secure new jobs, to demonstrate your competitiveness over your peers, to show your current employer that you are a proactive team member, or to introduce a new product or service for your business.

Watch this space

Social media is an ever-expanding and evolving area, so make sure you continually review what sites are best for you and whether this changes over time. Keep an eye on new social media networks that are relevant to your individual area of expertise and keep reviewing the type of people who frequent them – they can change quite quickly once a new or more relevant social network appears.

7.1   Some of the distribution tools at your disposal

Table 1: The tools at your disposal

In the following table we have outlined a few of the more popular and freely available social media tools. There are many resources available online to help you maintain a watch over a wide range of new and emerging social networks. Here are two different websites that provide an overview of social media networks:

▪ Wikipedia (**http://en.wikipedia.org/wiki/List_of_social_networking_websites**) is a great place to start for a simple list of social media sites.

▪ Traffikd (**http://traffikd.com/social-media-websites**) offers a list of categorised sites, which may help to identify appropriate sites for you, particularly if you are looking for a specific niche area from which to promote your personal reputation.

Table 7.1 The distributed tools at your disposal

Tool	Type	Ease of use
Facebook	Social network. Started off as a university *application*. Now wildly popular with 20 and 30-something students and professionals. Utilised by brands with devices like interest groups, brand pages, widgets and advertising. Recently added own name *URL* function which helps search engines to index an existing profile.	Very simple to get started or customise your existing profile with new content. For prospective employers, Facebook is an extremely popular tool to check whether an individual is serious, professional or creative.
MySpace	Social network. Generally used by the younger age groups (teenage and young adults) as 'a place for friends'. Used for connecting with friends, presenting personal profiles, blogs, joining groups, sharing photos, music, and videos.	Straightforward to set up a profile or change the privacy settings on an existing profile.

Ability to customise brand	Pros	Cons
If you already have a Facebook profile, one option is to label it 'Joe Bloggs personal' and set the privacy settings so it's closed to anyone not already a friend, then create a separate profile called 'Joe Bloggs work' or 'Joe Bloggs professional' to distinguish between the two personas. Afterwards, write on your wall that this is your professional profile and set the privacy settings as open to anyone searching on the internet, so you can be easily found.	1) The most popular social networking site so it offers good coverage. 2) Use your online framework from chapter six to help create sections. If you follow the 'work' approach, it might be slightly unconventional (Facebook is still primarily used to connect friends rather than work contacts), but it demonstrates that you are tech savvy and aware of maintaining a professional image. 3) Several brands are already on Facebook (not just through advertising but targeted groups e.g. Ernst & Young Careers.)	1) You will be judged in part by how your 'friends' are profiled, particularly if you do not separate your professional profile from your personal one. 2) Popular with users but still not seen by many as the 'professional' network. 3) Is seen by some employers as a timewaster during working hours.
Follow a similar process as used for Facebook to separate out your personal and professional life online.	1) Another very popular social network: 120 million active users, as of October 2008.[i] 2) Open and searchable by Google. 3) Popular with bands and artists, it's often associated with people who are more creative than users of other social networks (for instance, there's the option to add your favourite songs to your profile page).	1) You don't always know who you're dealing with as users don't have to reveal their name (although MySpace is trying to encourage people to do so). 2) There is an element of a popularity contest about MySpace; it could be viewed as a non-professional network by some.

Table 7.1 The distributed tools at your disposal

Tool	Type	Ease of use
Bebo	Social network.	Similar layout and ease of use in setting up or customising profile page as with MySpace and Facebook.
LinkedIn	Social network. Popular with professionals. Seen as the 'business' network.	Easy to set up your profile and customise it to suit your needs.

Ability to customise brand	Pros	Cons
Ability to follow the same process used for Facebook to separate out your personal and professional lives online.	1) Popular social network with more than 40 million members. 2) Open and searchable by Google.	1) The demographic of Bebo is considered to be younger than that of Facebook or MySpace so using it for work purposes might be less appropriate than using another social network. 2) Again, there's an element of a popularity contest about Bebo.
A profile page on LinkedIn is laid out like an online CV so importing your online framework under its headings is very straightforward.	1) LinkedIn has a reputation as a 'business social network', therefore, it is more likely to be used by your existing or future employer. 2) You can see the companies people work for and their past or current job titles. 3) Through connections it might be possible to gain access to influential people or potential employers more quickly than through other online means. 4) The power of recommendation is invaluable and is a recognised feature of this site.	1) As with other social networks, your brand will be judged in part by how many 'connections' you have on LinkedIn – is this how you want to be perceived? 2) It can take time to make new business contacts, gain a reputation for knowledge in a certain industry through LinkedIn groups or be recommended by another member. But then is that really so different to the offline world?

Table 7.1 The distributed tools at your disposal

Tool	Type	Ease of use
Flickr	Photo-sharing application.	Easy to set up a profile and upload photos.
Blogger	Blogging application owned by Google.	A blog can be set up in a couple of minutes using pre-defined templates and a Google ID.

Ability to customise brand	Pros	Cons
Very limited – although you can include a description in the 'describe yourself' box.	1) Ideal for anyone that wants to visually demonstrate their skills as the aim of Flickr is to upload photos and videos. 2) You can connect with others who might have similar interests or hobbies – a good way of demonstrating expertise in a particular area. 3) Can be used as a tool to promote new products or services by showing progress, images, text and so on.	1) This is a photo-sharing site so you're limited to expressing yourself solely by uploading photos or images.
You can use the 'profile' to describe yourself and break it down into specifics e.g. 'workplace', 'education' etc. Also, rather than creating chronological titles for archived blogs (e.g. January, February and so on), try using the online framework headings created in chapter six - Achievements, Status, Background and Interests (page 102) – to group blog posts thematically.	1) For those of you who prefer a simple, text-based layout in which to talk about yourself, a blogging application is ideal. 2) It's meant to be updated regularly, so it's easy to post blogs (no coding knowledge required) and you can post blogs from your mobile too. 3) Sure, there are millions of blogs nowadays, however, if you're using your blog to post intelligent articles – perhaps about an industry you want to get into or already work in to show in-depth knowledge – your blog will demonstrate to current or potential employers that you're serious about what you do or your intentions.	1) Blogs need to be updated regularly so don't choose this route if you don't plan to maintain or update your site regularly.

Table 7.1 The distributed tools at your disposal

Tool	Type	Ease of use
Worpress	Blogging application.	Quick and easy to set up an account, choose a template (of which there are plenty) and start blogging.
Twitter	*Microblogging application.*	Very simple to use and quick to get started. Simplicity of interface makes it easy to use on mobile phones.

Ability to customise brand	Pros	Cons
The site can be customised, although you are limited by the template design and one box for biographical information. However, as suggested for Blogger, you could use the blog to talk about yourself or write about subjects that are relevant to how you want to be perceived, then archive them by subject rather than date.	1) Simple to set up, text-based layout. 2) Easy to post blogs (no coding knowledge required). 3) As with Blogger, search engines will pick up your profiles as the site templates are generally well built and optimised, helping you to 'own' the first page of Google.	1) The same restrictions apply as for Blogger: blogs are only really useful if they are updated regularly.
Limited – only 140 characters to describe what you are doing, whether that's in your profile or through the updates that you post. You can customise the background and there are a growing number of templates you can use. You can also upload a custom background and more experienced users are already using this space to good effect to provide additional details (information, photo, logo, etc.) about themselves and their businesses.	1) It's a quick, easy-to-use application that lets you follow people or organisations of interest (Barack Obama has a Twitter feed, for example). 2) People can also follow you, so it's a good way of gaining a reputation for expertise in a subject or area.	1) One of the newer social media phenomena. Growing public awareness could result in overkill and then users moving away in droves to catch the next big thing (as with all social networks). 2) You only have 140 characters for each posting, so being concise is a pre-requisite.

Table 7.1 The distributed tools at your disposal

Tool	Type	Ease of use
YouTube	Video-sharing website.	Easy to become a member and upload videos.
Wikipedia	Online, *wiki*-based encyclopaedia.	Anyone can join Wikipedia and become an editor. In fact, every day hundreds of thousands of visitors from around the world collectively make tens of thousands of edits and create thousands of new articles.[iii] You can also create an article about yourself, as long as you have citable references to incorporate.

Ability to customise brand	Pros	Cons
You can give a description of yourself, your education and career history under the 'profile setup' section. There is also the ability to create a YouTube channel, perhaps to highlight your interests or your ability to present information clearly. YouTube, like Flickr, is a great tool to present video demos of your products or services.	1) A site with wide reach: YouTube attracted 100 million U.S. online video viewers in October 2008 alone.[ii] 2) Like Flickr or MySpace, YouTube is a good forum for sharing creative content, such as videos and blogs. 3) You can play YouTube videos on your website using the YouTube *widget* – a good way of joining up your online content across the web.	1) A lot of the content on YouTube is low quality, so it might not be the best forum for demonstrating your professionalism.
Edit down the *copy* you created under your four framework sections and use the same headings on your page. Unfortunately, the look and feel of the layout is limited to the template provided by Wikipedia.	1) Since its creation in 2001, Wikipedia has grown into one of the largest reference websites attracting at least 65 million visitors a month in 2009.[iv] 2) It looks impressive to have an encyclopedia entry about yourself. 3) Open and searchable by Google.	1) There's a dedicated group of editors so your Wikipedia posting may not remain online for very long if they don't consider it a worthy subject. 2) You must have citable references to include in your entry to demonstrate the legitimacy of the entry.

Table 7.1 The distributed tools at your disposal

Tool	Type	Ease of use
Knol	Google's online wiki-based encyclopaedia	You need a Google account to sign up and write a *knol*, but if you have already tried Blogger or use Gmail, you will have this already.

Ability to customise brand	Pros	Cons
As the author of a knol, you own the content. You can also use the settings to determine who has rights to edit the content.	1) Unsurprisingly, as it's a Google entity, Knol entries also appear in Google's search engine rankings (see the following chapter for more details).	1) Knol isn't as well known as Wikipedia so it may take time for your contributions to be acknowledged.
In addition, you can include a description of yourself in the profile section and import your own template.	2) As Knol isn't as established as Wikipedia, there's more chance of your entry lasting longer on Knol than it would on Wikipedia.	
	3) Knol has an advantage over Wikipedia in that the initial creator of the content or 'knol', owns the content. In Wikipedia, anybody can update content.	
	4) In January 2009, Google announced that Knol had grown to 100,000 articles, with users from 197 countries and territories visiting Knol on an average day.[v]	
	5) Knol has been designed to enable users to share their knowledge, so it's a great way of demonstrating your expertise in a subject or area.	

Other social media and tools

The table above lists the most popular and freely available social media tools, but there are plenty of others that may be more relevant to your circumstances or at different times in your career or professional life. These include Craigslist, eBay, Gumtree, Google video, Digg, Technorati and countless others (you can even create your own social network, using tools from providers such as Ning - **www.ning.com**, for example).

You might still choose to create a profile across several sites. If you do so, remember that you should maintain consistency. Social media sites are evolving entities, which means you will need to update and maintain your connections and profiles regularly.

7.2   Other distributed & social media tools

REPUTATION ACTION: CLEAN UP YOUR DIGITAL FOOTPRINT NOW

✔ If you already have multiple profiles on some of the social media sites now is the time to give them a spring clean. If you bear in mind that all of your digital profiles count towards the perception of your reputation, it's obvious that a consistent and professional representation of you and your brand could make all the difference.

Protecting your reputation across social media networks and websites

We've spoken quite a bit about promoting your brand across social media and other websites but what about protecting your reputation too?

Let's assume you have a group of friends or colleagues that are reasonably web and technically savvy. Are there any instances where they have uploaded stories, videos or pictures of you on the internet that you'd rather a recruiter or potential customer didn't see? It's a delicate area.

They may not be doing it maliciously – a friend could have posted pictures of you on Flickr or Facebook, for example – but there's no doubt that if the link is visible to search engines, then it's visible to potential customers or recruiters. And it could harm your reputation.

As it stands, the law says that if the photo belongs to them it is their copyright and you cannot claim any ownership of the image, even if it contains you. However, if they are a friend of yours, ask them if they'd mind removing it or changing the security settings on their social media space so it can't be viewed by a stranger. Most people will willingly help if they understand your concerns about it damaging your professional reputation.

Other possible issues you might face are a competitor for a job defaming you on Twitter or Facebook; other bloggers trying to close shop on a particular interest area; or a customer angry about the service he or she has received from you. Use your social media spaces website or blog to respond, correct falsehoods or engage in a two-way conversation. This is becoming an increasingly important reputation management issue; being aware of the issues and how to deal with them puts someone who's savvy about reputation management in the driving seat.

If that doesn't work, there are a number of other remedies to help you if a person or group of people has maliciously put up negative content about you on a social media space or website.

Generally, a polite 'would you mind' email or telephone call will do the trick; but if this doesn't help, there is legal recompense. It is not for the faint-hearted, nor is it cheap (see **Online Defamation** in chapter four, page 68). The direct action alternative is to continue to manage and enhance your online reputation and to 'knock' the negative comments further down the search engine listings – with positive results from your own website, social media profiles, blog, blog comments and so on taking their place instead. In fact, we'd advise you to do this, even if you go down the legal route.

A bit about blogging

Blogging is a simple and effective way to way to connect with your intended audience. The key to making the most of the blogging environment is to understand how the wider landscape works and to ensure you are utilising the right tools and techniques to show expertise, knowledge and maximise the visibility of your professional reputation.

Putting together a blog is immediate, simple and easy to set up:

1. Set up your own blog using free tools

Before you begin using blogs to promote your personal reputation, we can't stress enough how important it is to maintain a regular blogging schedule. If you want your blog to be read by relevant people and for them to find it in the first place, the content needs to be refreshed on a regular basis. The beauty of blogging is that you can talk about whatever interests you. Also remember to connect your blog back to the overall framework elements from chapter six (see **Step 3: Creating your online framework**, page 95), and you will have a

7.3 Free blogging tools are easy to use

ready-made, personalised 'super-CV' from which to promote and enhance your personal reputation.

There is no need to get technical with **web coding (See HTML coding)**, as blogging software does it all for you. The thing to focus on is the quality of the content. A good approach is to incorporate your four framework components into your main blog headings and then write away. Your blog should be viewed as an extension to your online profile, brand and reputation.

As part of an overall strategy, creating your own blog is one of the simplest ways to promote yourself online – and a great way to help people find the information that you want them to see about you. It also shows commitment, passion for your interest area and the ability to dedicate energy to a task. Your archive blogs will quickly grow into an interesting record for potential employers or customers – it shows you care about what you do and that you have been proactive in setting yourself up to talk confidently about what you can do.

TIP: WHY NOT INCLUDE KEY PHRASES IN YOUR BLOG HEADINGS OR CONTENT?

▸ Using key phrases and definitions like 'proactive employee', 'blogging project to show inventiveness', 'forward-thinking team member' or 'graduate seeking job blog' makes it easier for people to find you and also for the search engines to index your blogs.

▸ As part of your reputation managment strategy, plan your blog index so that when someone searches for you, some of the first page of google belongs to your blog. This will really help your reputation take off: no negative comments and plenty of mentions of you or your brand in different places – and all of them consistent, professional and directed towards your professional goals and objectives. To any potential employer or business contact this will look impressive.

2. Commenting on other people's blogs

It is important that you demonstrate awareness of what is happening in your industry. An hour or two spent searching for blogs that are relevant to your goals and getting involved in the subjects being debated will be time well spent for several reasons:

- It shows you are on top of what is happening and ahead of most other people in your industry.

- If you leave any comments on another person's blog (and if you have something worthwhile to say, you should) you can include a link back to your blog - this will increases trust in you as an interested and knowledgeable professional and begin to widen your sphere of influence, which by association enhances your reputation.

- Prospective employers or business contacts are also likely to read blogs in your industry, so if your name is consistently appearing as a source of help you will find it much easier to make an approach or ask for help yourself. It's also a great way to network online, and isn't that what reputation management is all about?

7.4   Commenting on other people's blogs is a good reputation strategy

A note of caution when commenting on other blogs:

Write your comment offline then go away from your computer. Take time to think how your comment may be perceived and if you are still happy then, by all means, post it. There have been far too many instances of people hitting 'send' in haste and regretting what they've written later. Remember, anything you post, comment on or write online can stay around for a very long time. So make sure it is something that will add to your reputation, not harm it.

Owning your own web space

Having control of a central hub to complement your social media profiles and blogs is a good way to effectively manage your online reputation.

With your own website, you can customise it in terms of how you want it to look, and only include information that you think is relevant (for example, several social networking sites insist on featuring your relationship details, but for a professional, work-focused website, such information is trivial at best or off-putting at worst).

7.5   A very simple web interface that presents information quickly

Most importantly, your own website is a place where you can centralise your reputation online. It's the hub for everything about you that you want people to find online about you. So even if you're using the other tools and don't mind updating content regularly across one or two key sites, we'd still recommend creating your own website for this vital reason.

Your personal reputation is your livelihood; your own web space gives you a competitive advantage in a tough marketplace.

Setting up your own website

This doesn't have to be as complicated as it sounds: you don't need any knowledge of HTML coding and you probably won't need to spend much money – if anything – in the process.

Choosing a name

It sounds obvious but keep your website name (otherwise known as a *domain name*) simple and, if possible, try to include your first name and last name eg. www.firstnamelastname.com. If this isn't available, don't despair. Just think a little creatively: try a combination of your first name, middle initial or middle name, then your surname. If this is also unavailable, try reversing your surname and first name and so on. If you still find they are all taken, try first name, last name, location or first name, last name, industry as follows:

www.joebloggsdesigner.com   or: www.joebloggslondon.com

Try and avoid the free internet names you see so often, like www.j1234.yahoo. com, as this shows that you haven't invested much time or effort in your personal reputation. It is really not that expensive to buy a relevant domain name and the impact it has can be well worth the investment.

Have a quick check now to see if your favoured website name is available, by simply typing the website address you'd like straight into your internet *browser*. If it returns an error page with 'no server found for this address', then the chances are it's available. Double-check by using a commercial service like **www.easily.com** or the internet registry **www.whois.org**. Again simply type in your preferred website name to see if it is available.

7.6 Search results for John Smith

It is also a good idea to search for your name on Google to see what results come up or who else might be competing against you for that name. If you're a graduate, perhaps also look up the names of other classmates to find out if they have a web presence. If you have a business, find out if your competitors' CEO, marketing director or COO has his or her own web presence. Do they come up in internet or social media searches? If you understand the strategies that your competitors are using (or not doing), you can plan your own strategy to maximise your personal reputation.

Don't just limit your search to the first three pages of Google, but explore down to page 10 or 12 so you have a good idea of what anyone searching on your name will find in the results.

The .com or .co.uk debate

You may find that your firstname.lastname choice for a website name is available in one domain rather than another e.g. .co.uk instead of .com.

This is because there are different levels of domains available around the world:

- .com is principally associated with the US and commercial organisations

- .co.uk is principally associated with the UK

- And in both territories, there are other, less well known domains such as .biz, org.uk, .me, .info, .net and .ac.uk

We would encourage you to choose either .com or .co.uk for your website. But whichever you choose, don't worry about buying more than one; you only need one domain for your website to come up in search engine listings. Buying several won't necessarily make you any more visible to the search engines.

Q. WHAT IF MY NAME HAS ALREADY GONE?

- Don't panic. Although having your first name and last name as your web address is the ideal situation (e.g. www.joebloggs.com), it's not the end of the world if someone else has already taken that name.

- There are plenty of ways of getting round the problem by using a derivative of your name. For example, try including middle initials, hyphens or underscores e.g. www.joejamesbloggs.com or www.joe-bloggs.com or www.joe_bloggs.com.

- Alternatively, switch the order of your name around e.g. www.bloggsjoe.com; add a description e.g. www.joebloggswebdesigner.com or a location e.g. www.joebloggslondon.com.

- However, don't include your date of birth in the domain name (e.g. www.joebloggs100278.com) for privacy and security reasons.

How to buy your domain name

You buy your domain name through a *'registrar'*. In the UK, this is a company that's registered with Nominet (the name of the body that hosts all .uk domain names). ICANN (**www.icann.org**) and InterNIC (**www.internic.com**) are global equivalents of Nominet, providing coverage for .com and other country domain names.

Most registrars are **Internet Service Providers (ISPs)** or specialist web companies, such as **UKReg.com** in the UK or **one.com**, which offers domain names on a global basis. They will often provide a bundled package of *web hosting* *(See Hosting)*, website software and combination of domain names for you (see **Hosting your website** for more information, page 142).

QUICK LINKS TO LOW COST DOMAIN AND ISP COMPANIES

+ **www.easily.com** – low-cost packages with pay-as-you-use hosting and easy to set up bundles

+ **www.123-reg.com** – constantly on the lowest cost domain names list, simple and effective service

+ **www.1and1.com** clear and direct domain name and hosting services

If you're just buying your domain name, search around for a good deal and expect to pay around £10 per year for a .com site; co.uk sites are quite a bit cheaper around £6 for two years. If the original search for your proposed domain name came up with a website offering to sell you the name, don't bother. It's not worth the money or hassle (see **What if my name has already gone?** for more information, page 137.)

Also, when searching for a domain name on a registrar's site such as **123reg.com** or **easily.com**, don't always go for the alternatives that they suggest if your first choice isn't available. Instead, you can always try one of the examples suggested in the section, **What if my name has already gone?** (page 137) which the registrar might not have recommended. Remember, it's your reputation, so you should choose the name that you think suits you best.

Make sure that you buy your domain name for at least two years and preferably 10 years. It will help raise your profile with search engines, which is how the majority of people will find your website in the first place.

For the same reason, you shouldn't let your domain name expire. It is a good practice to try to keep at least two years left on your purchase. It is frustrating – not to say expensive – to try and buy your domain name back from some of the more unscrupulous companies whose sole function is to buy up expired domain names for profit. Your website will also rank a lot higher in search engines as a result.

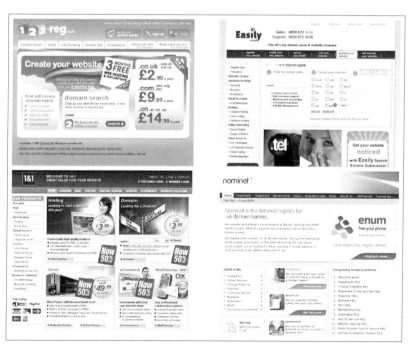

7.7 A selection of commercial domain name registrars

It might sound like a lot to remember when all we're talking about is your website name, but remember your name is your brand. So whether you go for www.joebloggs.com or www.joebloggslondon.com you should be looking to protect and nurture it, as it's your reputation that's on the line. Jobs, companies and environments come and go, but your good name is what sets you apart from everyone else, so it makes good business sense to protect it as much as you can.

CYBERSQUATTING

- This is the name given to a practice of buying a domain name with the intention of selling it on for inflated sums of money. For instance, a cyber squatter might buy a website name including a brand's trademark with the purpose of selling it to them at a later stage for more than the original asking price. It's illegal in the US under the Anti-cybersquatting Consumer Protection Act.

- If someone already has your name as their domain name, they're probably not cybersquatting. You might simply share a name and as domain names are provided on a first come, first served basis, they just got there first. But if you think someone is deliberately cyber-squatting, take it up with the relevant authority. ICANN and InterNIC both have processes in place to assist victims of cyber-squatting. A good first step if you believe you are a victim is to complete an InterNIC Registrar Problem Report (**http://reports.internic.net/cgi/registrars/problem-report.cgi**).

Added extras

When you're online, you need to be continually thinking about managing your reputation, even when considering small details like what email address to use. Your aim throughout is to ensure that anything you do online enhances your career and business prospects.

When you buy a domain name, you'll often receive a free email address for that website included as part of the package. We recommend you take advantage of this and give it a sensible name e.g. mail@joebloggs.com rather than joe@joebloggs.com as it sounds more professional. Remember, first impressions are just as important online as they are offline. So, which of these addresses sounds more professional to you: mail@fredbloggs.com or funnyjoebloggs76@hotmail.com?

If you prefer to use a webmail account and your service provider doesn't offer this facility, you can always direct any mail received through your website email address to your 'professional' webmail account, simply by changing the settings in your account.

TOP TIPS ON AVOIDING SPAM EMAIL

▶ Expect to get some *spam* if you put your email address on your website. Unfortunately, it's a fact of the internet that spammers exist and will target you with unnecessary emails – just as you might receive 'junk mail' in the post or an unwanted sales call on your phone.

▶ Online, spammers track new websites with a view to finding new email addresses. For this reason, some people choose not to include their email address on their site. However, if you think the benefit outweighs the irritation of receiving spam emails, set your spam filter to 'high' to try and minimise the amount of spam you receive in your inbox.

▶ Another remedy is to list your email address as mail AT joebloggs.com which will prevent spam phishers picking up your email address. People will understand that 'AT' is the same as '@'.

▶ Be aware of identity theft online. It's a growing threat[vi] but there are ways to minimise your exposure – just as you don't leave your valuables on display when you leave your car parked overnight, you can reduce your chances of being affected.

TOP TIPS ON AVOIDING SPAM EMAIL (CONT.)

▸ One thing we'd suggest if you're setting up an email address such as mail@joebloggs.com that is publicly available on the internet through your website, is to use a different, more private email address for transactions that require more security, such as online banking. When you buy a domain name you're often provided with more than one email address, so take advantage of this feature to add a bit of extra protection around your identity e.g. use bank@joebloggs.com only for your online banking details.

▸ It is a good idea to set up your 'public' email address as 'mail' or 'info' or 'sales', so if a spammer or hacker tries to access information from your bank they won't have the correct email address to start with – just don't ever let anyone know you use these aliases.

▸ With all this talk about setting up multiple email accounts, you might now be thinking that this is going to be a lot of extra effort to manage. Don't worry, it's not. You can set up your email accounts so that all emails ultimately end up in one place – your 'public' email account (eg mail@joebloggs.com) and you can see which email address you were initially contacted through.

Hosting your website

Once you've bought your domain name and set up your email address, the next step is finding somewhere to host your website.

If you're connected to the internet through an Internet Service Provider (ISP) the chances are your account provides you with some free storage where you can host your website. Alternatively, your website software might come with some as standard (for instance, the MobileMe service from Apple includes hosting space on Apple's servers).

Or perhaps when you bought your domain, it came with some free web space and instructions for uploading content to your website. There are numerous providers of these bundled packages, such as **www.123-reg.com**, so search around for the best package to suit your needs. These packages can be bought for as little as a few pounds a month.

Building your website

Now you need to build your website. This isn't as tricky as it sounds; nor does it require much IT knowhow.

If you use an Apple Mac, you will most likely have an application already installed called iWeb. If you use a Microsoft Windows PC you are unlikely to have similar software already on your PC but there are plenty of free website packages available online, try typing 'free website software' or 'free *content management package (See Content Management System)*' into Google or Yahoo!. You may even get a web software bundle as part of your hosting/domain name package. Alternatively there are several commercial 'website in a box' packages available that do the same job for around £40 and upwards.

Whichever route you choose, investing in your own domain name and a simple, easy-to-navigate website are powerful tools to help you promote your online reputation.

Don't fall into the common trap of thinking that your website has to contain lots of moving images or flashing signs on the homepage, it doesn't. What's important is that you have a web presence in the first place with quality content, which projects the image of 'you' that you want people to discover.

Content for your website

This is the easy part, as all you're doing is loading up content you created earlier to the website template. Through the exercises listed in the previous chapter, you should already have decided what you want to say and how to structure the content.

Use the same headings – Achievements, Status, Background and Interests – as page titles and populate the sections with the content you've listed under each.

Joe Bloggs

Joe Bloggs   Current Role   Previous Employment   Qualifications   Interests   Halpern Cowan   Sitemap

Joe Bloggs

Joe Bloggs
Current Role
Previous
Employment
Qualifications
Interests
Halpern Cowan
Sitemap

Quisque sed ipsum eget erat faucibus aliquet? Phasellus volutpat facilisis augue sit amet adipiscing. Nunc at ante sem, ac ultrices sem? Sed vehicula mollis est a pretium. Vivamus at nisl vel nisl dapibus vulputate. Maecenas non scelerisque purus! Suspendisse neque massa, ultricies at malesuada id, tincidunt quis massa. Mauris sed urna nisi. Integer at ligula diam, vitae dictum nibh.

Nullam luctus convallis massa nec aliquet. Fusce odio leo, tempus pulvinar euismod sit amet; feugiat id leo. In porta mauris a dolor porta in interdum lacus venenatis. Ut nulla quam, malesuada viverra tristique ut, commodo quis lectus. Aliquam neque dui, adipiscing sed sagittis id, auctor ut nisl. Sed tincidunt tempor tristique. Suspendisse tincidunt; leo quis ultricies dictum, felis quam mattis lectus, nec imperdiet lectus ligula vel massa? Integer ultrices, ligula non aliquet elementum, erat lacus accumsan nulla; eget feugiat odio leo ac enim. Suspendisse porta pretium neque, cursus pretium elit pharetra ut.

7.8   An example of a simple personal website

It will take a little bit of time but you can always revisit and amend the copy later on if your circumstances change.

Include simple tricks: use headers, sub-headers, pull-out quotes, all the things that make reading about you and your brand interesting. People on the internet read in a very different way to how they read newspapers or books, and their attention span is typically much shorter. You've already done the hard work by getting them to your site, now make it easy for them to read what's on it:

- Use clear and simple navigation to help users get around your site;

- Break content sections down into small easily-readable chunks;

- Use headings and sub-heading to make scanning clear and effective;

- Don't let lines exceed 12-14 words, as it is hard to read across any farther and it leads to eyestrain (and a potential new employer or recruiter clicking off your profile to someone else's site that is easier to read and navigate);

- Ensure your basic contact details are easy to find – there is nothing more frustrating for a busy professional than liking what they see but not finding any way of getting in touch with you.

Google describes you in 20 words

Google doesn't give you many words to get your message across on the search results page. So your short executive summary of around 20 words needs to be punchy, direct and relevant, as you will only get seconds to make an impact on a prospective employer or business contact. The *page title* from your website will be the first thing your prospective employer or client will see so make sure it's relevant. Here are some examples:

New jobseekers
Remember that your online framework can easily be applied to your own website. Your intended audience want to find out about you, so have some fun, sell yourself and your interests, and give the reader an insight into your personality.

Consider if you were an employer looking for a graduate and you came across the following search result after looking up a candidate. Would you be intrigued to find out more?

A POWERFUL GOOGLE DESCRIPTION

* **John Smith Exciting New Graduate** – Keen, innovative, technology graduate using search techniques to help gain a first foothold in a technology company. Find out more here. Available September.

Above all, make sure the content is interesting. A prospective employer has a bundle of 'possibles' on their desk, so you need to stand out from the crowd. 5,000 words about how you spent a great summer in Africa before abandoning your studies won't necessarily endear you to them. Keep uppermost in your mind that your website is all about promoting your personal reputation.

Think 'what am I all about?' and 'what image do I want to project to potential readers?' when writing your content sections. Be direct in stating your strengths and describing what you are looking for in a role and what you have to offer ahead of the competition.

Don't be afraid to talk up your skills and knowledge. There will be any number of people competing against you for that next step up the ladder or first job opportunity, so use your website to the maximum effect and both your next employer and the search engines will be able to find you easily.

Business professionals

Your previous background can help to enhance your reputation. Credibility, trust, innovation, customer service and your own work achievements should form the cornerstone of the content on your central web space. Obviously, include your personal goals and achievements too, as this all helps to build up a picture of you for any potential customers, shareholders or business contacts.

When you've been working for several years, it can be hard to distinguish between what you do and 'you'. So think about how you can use your website to build up a picture of your own achievements within the sphere of your company and demonstrate the knowledge or expertise you have built up over the years.

For example, elements of your website content could take the form of a diary of events for a new product launch, highlighting where you will be available to discuss business at forums, seminars or online on social networks – or even how you are using the internet as a key tool in developing proactive, two-way communications.

The key point for business professionals is to manage your reputation through how you personally influence decisions within your company and how you have in the past. Interested parties such as new customers or clients will then be able to see a direct connection between what your company offers and what you offer. It connects the human 'you' to the business 'you'.

Why Google loves your business executive summary:

Here's an example of a good Google organic search result that ties in an executive summary and comes across as personal and professional:

A POWERFUL GOOGLE DESCRIPTION

✦ **John Smith CEO** – My personal mission is to get closer to our customers and find out how we can improve our services. Contact me personally at www.johnsmithceo.com

This is what customers will see when they type 'John Smith' into Google. A punchy, relevant and unique description that not only ensures Google indexes your site and considers it relevant, but also that your customers do too.

Would you click on that link if you had met John Smith CEO and were considering using his company for a large contract?

Finally, don't treat your website as an isolated entity. Many social media sites let you download applications that link directly to your profile on their site from your website. So use these applications (generally known as widgets) as an opportunity to join up your online presence, while ensuring that the image you portray across each site is consistent.

Tricks of the trade

▪ Remember not to write too much copy for each section. Keep the content limited to 250 words at most and at least 1,000 words across the entire site. You also don't want to create too many web pages, so when you're starting out, look to build five pages initially (a homepage, plus one for each of the framework headings from chapter six, page 102.)

▪ Don't overcomplicate things – you don't need an all-singing, all-dancing website. If the content is relevant, people will find it regardless of what the site looks like.

▪ Check that all spelling and grammar across the site is correct. Nothing shouts amateur more than poor diction.

- Keep reminding yourself about the internet and how people use it in the way you structure your website e.g. in your use of headlines, etc.

- Check all the links on your site work, whether they are internal links to other pages, or links to useful and relevant external websites such as your social media spaces, otherwise it will look unprofessional.

- If you're using images, resize them so they're smaller and optimised for the web. Remember, you want your site to load quickly, and not everybody is on super-fast broadband yet, so don't overload your site with too many large images or media files.

What if you already have a website?

If you already have a website, we don't expect you to abandon it and start again from scratch. After all, you have carried out some of the important legwork already, such as finding a name for your website, developing navigation, *building links (See Link Building)*, and creating content.

Instead, check that it corresponds with the principles of good web design practice that we've outlined above. The main rule is to keep it simple: you are not trying to win any design awards, you just want to create a consistent, positive profile to put you at the forefront of recruiters', employers' and customers' minds.

Also, clean up your digital footprint by checking that your branding is consistent across all the sites where you have a presence – and in particular, on social media sites. This includes re-checking your privacy settings on those sites to ensure that only the information you are happy for people to find out about you is publicly available online.

Q. IF I ALREADY WORK FOR A COMPANY AND I'M NOT LOOKING FOR A JOB, ISN'T REPUTATION MANAGEMENT UNNECESSARY?

* Answer: Not at all. In fact, quite the opposite. Personal reputation management is all about the benefit you can bring to your company. It enhances the professional profile of your company by showing how the people who work in the company are proactive and forward thinking.

* After all, companies are made up of people, and it's people that employers, customers or contacts are interested in. It also shows your employer that you are taking an interest in improving your and your company's reputation, so if anything, it should only work in your favour.

Q. YOU'VE BEEN TALKING A LOT ABOUT PERSONAL WEBSITES, BUT WHAT ABOUT MY COMPANY WEBSITE, IS THAT REDUNDANT?

* Answer: No, your company website is still a major starting point for staff, customer enquiries, newemployees and so on. Think of it this way: Google and the other major search engines is now the gateway to you or company. People these days are just as likely to type company or individual names directly into a search engine box rather than trying to second-guess a company's web address, further highlighting the importance of having a relevant website domain name.

Q. YOU'VE BEEN TALKING A LOT ABOUT PERSONAL WEBSITES, BUT WHAT ABOUT MY COMPANY WEBSITE, IS THAT REDUNDANT? (CONT.)

+ And, as you by now know, what people find on the search engines has a major impact on what action they take next. What would you do if you searched for a prospective employment opportunity at an exciting new company and found nothing but negative comments?

Final thoughts

Beginning to manage your online reputation will pay dividends if you utilise tools that are already available online. Remember to be consistent in what you say: decide what your main goal and objective is (e.g. get a new job, increase your customer base, show your existing employer that you are proactive and so on), and use whichever tools are suitable for you personally to reinforce the message continuously.

KEY LEARNINGS FROM THIS CHAPTER

■ There are multiple channels from where you can promote your online reputation.

■ A mix of social media, blogs and your own website is a powerful combination, and makes you visible to your target audience and to search engines.

■ Review social media sites to ascertain which of those are relevant for you.

- Begin to clean up your digital footprint by separating out the personal information from the professional information in your social media profiles.

- Maintain consistency across social media sites and update your connections and profiles regularly.

- Use your online framework from chapter six to create your key content across social media networks, blogs and your own website.

- Pick a simple tool such as Blogger or Wordpress to get your blog started.

- Pick a blogging schedule (say, twice a week) and stick to it.

- Read blogs in your industry or sector, comment on them, and link them back to your blog, profile or website – people who are interested in your area read these blogs and this includes recruiters and potential customers.

YOUR WEBSITE

- Creating your own website gives you a place where you can centralise your reputation online.

- Find a free or cheap package on the internet or buy a domain with a free simple website package to keep costs low.

- Keep your website name simple and try to include your first name and last name eg. www.firstnamelastname.com.

- Choose either .com or .co.uk for your website, but don't worry about buying more than one domain.

- Make sure that you buy your domain name to last for at least two years (preferably 10) and set up a reminder to renew it six months in advance of its expiry date.

- Use the 'big four' professional statement headings – Achievements, Status, Background and Interests – as page titles and populate the sections with the content you've listed under each.

- Don't treat your website as an isolated entity. Many social media sites let you download applications that link directly to your profile on their site from your website. So use these applications (otherwise known as 'widgets') as an opportunity to join up your online presence, while ensuring that the image you portray across each site is consistent.

Your online reputation status

By now you've developed your online framework, looked into a strategy for presenting yourself online and have a consistent and professional online presence across social media sites, your blog and your own website.

The next thing we need to look at is what you need to do to get you noticed by the two key groups who can make a difference to your objectives: your intended audience and the major search engines.

Up next:
Getting people, search engines and social networks to notice you

8

Getting people, search engines and social networks to notice you

In this chapter, you will:

- Find out about how search engines 'view' your websites
- Understand the simple techniques that will help you to achieve better visibility
- Use a simple step by-step process to maximise all your hard work in creating relevant content that people can find

The four most important things to get you noticed are:

Consistency: Develop your reputation story and use the vast connected world to help people find it.

Content: Make your content relevant and punchy, and connect page titles, headings and copy together.

Indexing: Index your site on the main search engines in less than 30 minutes.

Linking: Building links to quality people, networks and web spaces.

By now you have the tools and techniques necessary to set up and use blogs and social media sites, not to mention creating your own website. You have written your 'big four' professional statements as part of your online framework, and you have ensured that you are consistently portrayed across multiple digital touchpoints.

But can you assume the work is now done and your online reputation is in good hands?

Not quite...

Try it for yourself: type your name into Google. Does the website that you have created appear in the first three pages? What about when you type the actual URL of your website into the search engine of Google, Yahoo! or Live Search (Microsoft's search engine), does it come up then?

Unless you have a particularly unique name, the answer is probably not. Unfortunately, it's not enough just to create a web space online; more importantly, you need to get noticed by the search engines so that when recruiters or potential customers come searching for you, they only find the information that you are personally managing, which shows you in the best possible light.

Similarly how do you become more visible on the social networks, in the *blogosphere*, Twitter, Wikipedia or other areas that are relevant to you and your brand?

In this chapter, we'll explore the ways in which you can ensure your content is found by the search engines and – equally importantly – by the people you are targeting. We'll also include some professional tips and tricks to further boost your visibility online.

The power of search engines (and how you can harness it – because most people won't bother)

Search engine experts can talk forever about complex search engines algorithms, *backlinks*, page titles and how these are crucial to the success of your website's visibility. Unfortunately, it's when people use these phrases that most people's eyes start to glaze over and they start wishing that they were on a beach somewhere with a pina colada close at hand and a copy of their favourite book.

To most people, the art of *search engine optimisation* just isn't that interesting. However, understanding the basics and using these techniques and skills to manage your online reputation is advantageous. Your secret weapon is that most people simply won't bother to do the same, giving you a headstart over competitors and peers.

A stark fact about search engines is that however relevant, however good, the copy is on your site or blog, if your site hasn't been indexed (which tells the search engine that your site exists) all your hard work will go unnoticed when a recruiter, customer or contact searches under your name. Worse still, people with the same name could be taking your business or your job right from under your nose. The good news is that making your central website visible to the search engines is a simple task to complete.

UH-OH, IT'S GETTING TECHNICAL...

+ What we're talking about might sound a little complicated, but stick with us, as you are well on the way to developing your personal reputation online.

Bad karma

You could, of course, go ahead and buy up your competitors' domain names, bid for search terms under their *keywords*, cyber-squat or undertake any number of other legal but morally dubious techniques. But wouldn't you rather concentrate on developing a robust, clear and consistent reputation for yourself? It is ten times easier for your audience to understand what you are all about and much better for you, than to waste energy on badmouthing someone else's reputation or company.

How to make your website or blog easy to find by search engines

We recommend indexing your web spaces on the three main search engines: Google, Yahoo! and Live Search as these constitute around 90 per cent of searches conducted on internet search engines.[i]

To add your URL (or domain name) to Google, simply type into the search engine input box 'add URL to Google' (you don't need the quotation marks). URL stands for Uniform Resource Locator and it's effectively the address of your website on the web.

In the Google search engine results, you'll see a weblink to the 'add URL' page. Don't worry about the other search results, many of which are for sites offering to do the job for you on all the major search engines for a price (see below). You don't need to index your site on all of them, especially as Google, Yahoo! and Microsoft dominate the UK and US markets.

Next, click onto the link **http://www.google.com/addurl/?continue=/addurl** and follow the instructions on the page (for example, including the http:// part of your website address, where requested). Where it asks for a description of the site (Google does, for example) include a brief description of yourself e.g. 'Joe Bloggs, web designer southwest London'. Don't bother with conjunctions like 'is', 'and' etc., just keep it brief and succinct.

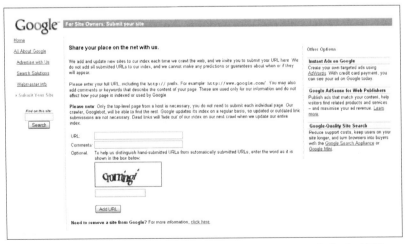

8.1 The Google add URL page

Follow the same procedure for Yahoo! and Live Search.

For Yahoo!, visit: **http://siteexplorer.search.yahoo.com/submit** and follow the instructions (it's very similar to Google).

For Live Search, go to: **http://search.msn.com/docs/submit.aspx?FORM=WSUT** and enter in your URL – not forgetting the prefix http://.

Other search engines including AOL and Ask Jceves can be considered too; just follow the same procedures outlined above, bearing in mind that these less popular search engines don't have the same reach as the other three.

If you want to use one of the sites available on the internet offering to do the indexing job for you (usually for a fee, although some are free), be careful that your chosen provider doesn't spam the search engines with requests – this will have the opposite effect to the one you want! Search for 'submit URL' on any of the main search engines to obtain a list of companies who offer this service.

Making your content relevant to search engines

To most people, how search engines work is still regarded as something of a dark art. But if you keep your website copy relevant and punchy, and follow some of the simple techniques we suggest below, it will pay dividends for your online reputation.

Each of the search engines operates slightly differently, but essentially they rely on complex algorithms to 'crawl' the web and deliver the most accurate results for a user's request. For this reason, you want to ensure that the copy included on your site helps increase your position in search engine results if someone is searching for your name (or even something related, such as 'web designer, southwest London').

You might think you've already done this by building a site based on your 'big four' pillars, so your site only includes information that you want people to find out. However, there are some extra technical adjustments you can make to the copy, which will improve your presence in a search engine's results page and make it easier for people to find you, helping to make your professional reputation more visible.

How to ensure what you write helps your search engine position

Page titles

You may have noticed when you visit a website that each webpage has some text at the very top of the web browser.

Visit the BBC's website (**www.bbc.com**), for example, and it says at the top of the page '*BBC | Homepage*'. This is the page title for this web page. If you click on the News link on the BBC homepage, the page title for the News section is different: '*BBC NEWS | News Front Page*'. On one of the BBC's newsbeat pages the following message is displayed:

8.2 Page titles from the BBC website

The point is that the page title should give a clear outline of each page's content to make it easy for the search engines to understand how relevant the content contained within that page is. Techniques such as this can help your site to appear higher in the search engines listings when someone searches for you.

8.3 Page titles from Apple, The Times and Sainsbury's

REPUTATION ACTION: PAGE TITLES

✔ Go back to your online framework from chapter six and review the content on each page to come up with individual page titles. Try to be concise and explain what the page is all about in about 8-10 words. Try a format like:

- Your Name – Your page – Page description for each of the main sections.

✔ Make sure that you fill in the page title of each page as this is what search engines use first of all to search and define your website. Keep it simple and use a similar description to that used when adding your URL. For example, if your website is www.joebloggs. com, give the page title for the homepage as 'Joe Bloggs – web designer, southwest London'. For your Achievements section, consider a page title of 'Joe Bloggs – Achievements'.

✔ The tool that you've used to create your website should have some options to enable you to easily update your page titles.

Main copy

On each page of your website, make sure your name is included once in the main copy of each page. Don't use it repeatedly, however, as this can be considered excessive by the search engines (see next page).

An ideal amount of copy on each page is between 250 and 500 words. This gives each page credibility and gives you a chance to explain to the reader what the site or page is all about. If you are including CV type information on your website – perhaps you are a first jobber or need to use this type of format – consider including it as an Adobe PDF file.

Don't forget, people may want to print out information about you, so where you have too much text to fit on a page (such as a CV, product information, technical specs and so on), consider offering this as a download from your site in PDF format. It always makes more sense from a search engine and usability perspective to keep the information on your main web space succinct, offering the option to download more information if required.

Things you shouldn't do when writing your website copy

Search engines aren't stupid. In fact, they rely on highly intelligent technology, which is designed to improve the accuracy and relevance of search engine results for users. What this means is they don't like sites that pretend to be something they're not, so transparency in how you present content on your site is key.

You might not think that you're doing anything wrong in trying to increase your site's visibility, but there are some things you really shouldn't do as they will actually have a very detrimental effect on your website's visibility on search engines, not to mention your own personal reputation. So steer well clear of these techniques and of any companies or individuals who suggest you use them:

Repeating your name frequently on each page – You want people to find your site using your name, and your name is regarded as a 'keyword' by search engines. So while it's a good idea to include your name at least once in the main copy on each page, don't overstep the mark and use it repeatedly in the hope that it will increase your position in search engine results. It won't; instead, search engines will regard your website as spam and downgrade your subsequent results ranking. What this means is your site will be less likely to be found when someone searches on your name or company – defeating the purpose of managing your reputation.

A simple rule of thumb to follow is don't use any techniques or write anything that your wouldn't feel comfortable an employer or business contact knowing about - always protect your good name at all costs.

IF YOU HAVE THE NECESSARY EXPERIENCE TO EDIT YOUR PERSONAL WEBSPACE WITH HTML

+ Don't include hidden links on a page when you're building the website – a hidden link will be invisible to a human eye, but visible to a search engine. Links or text can be hidden in various ways – using the same colour as the background so it can't be seen by the naked eye, for example. Search engines view this practice as spam and consequently your website won't be included in their results.

+ Don't use 'doorway pages' – These are web pages that contain repeated use of keywords to increase a site's ranking on a search engine. They're only visible to search engines, and are designed to act as a 'doorway' through to another web page. BMW's German website was blacklisted by Google after it was found to have used this practice to ensure a higher search ranking when users searched for 'used car'.[ii] There are plenty of dubious companies out there who will offer shortcuts to get your name to the top of Google's search engine rankings. But remember, it's much better to take time and focus on building your personal reputation consistently and with transparency.

▲▲ It takes many good deeds to build a good reputation, and only one bad one to lose it. ▼▼ [iii]

Benjamin Franklin

Search engines will take a very dim view if you try using any of these 'tricks' and you could find that you're *'blacklisted'*, which is very bad news for your reputation. If you are in doubt about anything you're thinking about doing or someone else has suggested, check the search engine's webmaster guidelines to see what they will allow, such as **http://www.google.com/support/webmasters/bin/answer.py?hl=en&answer=35769**

While we're suggesting useful resources, check out **www.searchenginewatch.com**. It's one of the most established search news and resources sites, and contains a lot of good articles and suggestions about all aspects of search engine visibility.

Q. WHAT DOES IT MEAN IF MY WEBSITE IS 'BLACKLISTED' BY THE SEARCH ENGINES?

* If your site is blacklisted by a search engine, it means that your site may have done something that contravenes the search engine's guidelines. This might be anything from appearing to 'spam' through the use of too may keywords on each page; or in more extreme situations, it could be infringing copyright, using inappropriate language, containing adult content etc. Blacklisting does not necessarily mean your site will be removed from the index, but it will fall in rankings as any links to the site will be removed.

* Research company, Hitwise, tracked the impact on GoCompare.com, a price comparison site for insurance, of being blacklisted by Google. Apparently the search engine had uncovered some "irregular inbound links to its site." While Hitwise analyst, Robin Goad, noted that the site was the number one result in the non-paid-for search engine results, once it had been blacklisted it dropped down to the seventh page of listings.

- To put this into context, Goad observed that during the week ending 26 January 2008, GoCompare captured 17.49 per cent of all search traffic from the search term

  'car insurance'. By the week ending 9 February 2008, after it had been blacklisted, it was only receiving 2.31 per cent of all search traffic using the same search term. Its competitors, meanwhile, saw their traffic increase significantly.[iv]

- This could be your reputation on the line. Whether it was intentional or not, blacklisting can have a dire effect on your online reputation. If you are not comfortable with any advice you are being given on optimising your web space, err on the site of caution and do some further research using reputable industry sources before proceeding.

Why links are important

Indexing your site and making the content of your site relevant to search engines are two necessary steps in getting your site noticed and getting the people you want to notice you interested. They're not enough on their own however, to guarantee you a spot in the top three pages of Google and other search engines.

Indexing only makes sure your site is listed in the search engine's 'library'; it won't give you a higher ranking in the results. It can also take up to six months to become effective.

So you need to consider a third important step: building relevant links between your site and other websites.

Building links will help to improve your website ranking in search engine results, as the more quality *inbound links* you have, the more likely it is that the search engine gives you a higher ranking, making your site easier to find. This is because search engines are, in essence, a big popularity test. The most popular sites rise to the top of search engine results pages faster than those with fewer quality links.

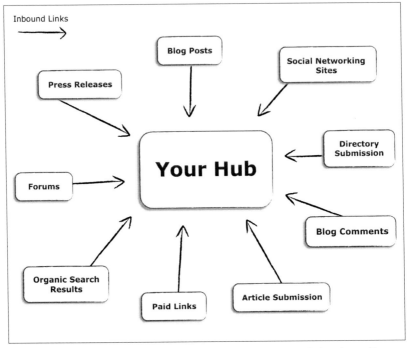

8.4 Build your links through reputable sources

WHAT ARE GOOD AND BAD LINKS

- Before you start chasing links from every website available, you need to understand that some links are more valuable than others.

- This is because relevancy has a part to play in how search engines rank your website. So web links from sites that are particularly relevant to your site are of a higher quality than links from an unrelated source. For example, if you are John Smith, a small accountancy business owner, a link from the local chamber of commerce website will be more relevant for your site than a link from a local hairdresser's site.

- You also want any sites that you're linking with to rank highly on Google. In turn, this will help increase your rankings on the search engine.

- Working out how high a particular *page ranks (See Search ranking)* on Google isn't as difficult as it sounds. All you need to do is download the Google toolbar, which you can find through the search engine or by visiting **www.toolbar.google.com**.

8.5   Google Toolbar with PageRank

- The toolbar is easy to download and works with PCs and Macs, so there should be no problem with the software being incompatible with your computer. The download takes a matter of minutes – depending on the speed of your internet connection – and once it's installed, you will be able to see the Google toolbar whenever you load up your internet browser.

WHAT ARE GOOD AND BAD LINKS (CONT.)

■ To find out how a page is ranked by Google – essentially how important Google considers the page to be – look for the 'page rank' widget on your browser (it is generally located in the bottom right corner of the Firefox browser or in the menu bar of the Internet Explorer browser). This is a green bar that ranks a site between zero and 10. Every time you visit a new website, the page rank will change depending on its Google ranking. For example, the page rank of **www.google.com** is eight out of ten.

■ What you're looking for when building links are sites that have a *page ranking* of one or above, as this means that not only has it been indexed by Google but that it is also visible to the search engine technology that determines where it appears in the results page of a search.

■ Another way of checking how popular a website is and, therefore, how valuable a site it will be to link with – is to use a website called **Alexa.com**, which collects information on web usage. Under the 'Traffic Rankings' section, you can type a URL or website name into the 'lookup box', which will produce statistics about the number of people visiting the site from around the world and where this puts the site in the popularity stakes. You may even find that if you've installed the Google tool bar, the Alexa Page Rank widget appears in your browser also.

■ Don't be surprised if a site you're thinking of linking with doesn't appear in the results; Alexa's site only ranks the most popular one million sites around the world. In which case, the Google page rank might be a more reliable measure of a site's usefulness to you.

REPUTATION TIP

▶ Don't go crazy worrying about website page ranks to the detriment of linking your site with other professionals and businesses in your particular area; people with complementary skills can be far more useful in spreading the word about who you are and what you do. It's useful to check the links of those people or companies you're unfamiliar with, but remember, it's what they do and how their site can complement your site that's most important.

Where to find links for your site

Friends and colleagues – If they have their own website ask them to include a link to your site. Do the same if they have a blog – or consider asking them to write a blog post on you.

However, avoid including a link to their site, if possible. It might seem unfriendly, but *reciprocal links* cancel one another out so the advantage for your site will be lost.

New connections – Links from friends' sites might be the easiest to obtain, but remember, the most valuable links are those that are relevant to what you do. So look for people with common interests: industry bodies, associations, even your trade union or workplace could have a website that you can link your site to.

Another way of building up quality links for your website is to comment on stories that are relevant to content on your website, so perhaps stories about finding an accountant on Digg (**www.digg.com**) if you work in that profession would be relevant.

Make sure you use the same keywords and name that you use on your website for consistency of message, as well as a link on the comment back to your own website, blog or social media space – whichever you've decided is the main hub for your reputation information. Also, only comment on blogs or sites where you can see the names of the other people who have commented and their website links, as this suggests it's a more trustworthy source. Commenting will also help build up your reputation as an 'expert' in your chosen subject area.

Q. CAN I USE SOCIAL NETWORKS OR BLOGS TO GET MYSELF NOTICED BY THE SEARCH ENGINES RATHER THAN MY WEBSITE?

- Yes. Using blogs and social media sites is a great way to show the widest possible audience who you are and what you offer. Search engines will also index your social media spaces and blogs.

- Our recommendation is that you create all three elements as part a complementary online reputation strategy. However, creating your own website is often the quickest and most visible way for the search engines to find your content.

- One problem with focusing on a particular social network or social media tool is that over time it could be superseded by a new network with more people and features, causing a subsequent reduction in search result rankings.

- There is also the issue of dilution. If you are continually setting up profiles on new networks simply to maintain currency, you will find that as a result, even though your digital footprint will increase, there will be more pages to clean up, look after and access, to the point that it becomes unmanageable.

However, if you do want to use one of the widely available social media tools, here are some steps to getting your reputation noticed:

Being visible on... Facebook

▪ Don't forget that Facebook profiles appear in search engine results (albeit generally a little slower) as much as individual web pages, so you need to ensure that what's visible is what you'd want people to read or see about you.

▪ Remember to use your real name. It sounds obvious, but it's often overlooked. A username of Johncrazyguy999 isn't going to endear you to any recruiters in the near future. Use your real name and stick to it in all your professional dealings.

8.6 A public profile on Facebook

Being visible on... LinkedIn

▪ As one of the more popular 'business' social networks, a careful selection of business-related keywords will help you to be found on this social network.

▪ As with all things relating to one of your most important assets – your reputation – consistency, quality and relevance are essential.

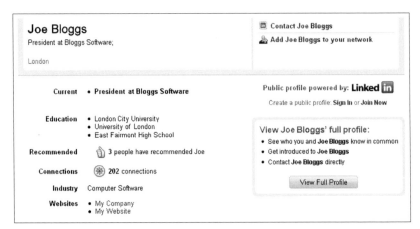

8.7 A LinkedIn profile

Being visible on... Twitter

▪ Reputation savvy individuals are using this simple form of communication to make their job hunt, business idea, or even quality of customer service extremely visible to an audience of receptive and forward-thinking professionals. Just remember to keep your message succinct so it fits within the required 140 characters. Keep your communications brief but repeat it often and make it relevant to your audience to get noticed.

8.8 A public profile on Twitter

Ideas for increasing your visibility

Idea 1: You are a business owner with a new product idea

Use Twitter to help you refine your idea by engaging customer feedback. 'Tweet' other people working in your industry to ask their opinions on what you're developing and create new contacts. Consider beginning a diary to update on the product or service offering, letting people know when *beta* versions are available for testing – and using the power of connections to garner product and brand advocates from the outset.

Use your other business and professional profiles to help spread the word about the new product: use Flickr for screen shots of your products, LinkedIn to enquire about co-funding, and so on. Use your personal blog to tell the story of the launch, and Twitter to inform your followers of relevant updates or releases and to announce the product launch.

Consider setting up a competition for help with marketing a strapline for the product or testing its viability. Centralise all of your findings, ideas and progress on your website - using your online framework as a guide.

Idea 2: You are looking for a new job

Use Twitter to tell the story of your job hunt: follow recruiters and HR professionals using Twitter Search. Comment on their tweets, retweet anything you find interesting, and tweet them with updates on your job search or to ask for advice or help.

Over time, you will gain more followers as more and more people work out how your job search is getting on. Tweet a few times a day to let them know any progress, and include any tips or techniques that prove effective. Also, blog about it on your other social media networks and blogs on an ongoing basis.

Consider using the story of your job hunt as part of your executive summary on your centralised web space. Put 'follow me on Twitter' with a link to your Twitter profile on every CV you send, not to mention your Facebook or LinkedIn profiles Soon you will begin to see how the internet consists of a wide-ranging connection of people, interests and common themes that you can tap into to build your own reputation.

Using social media to promote your reputation is all about centralising these themes and sticking to them. Your story may change over time – when you have found a new job or a new challenge, for example – but the core information remains the same. People are interested in people, let them find you and you will start to see the benefit of managing your reputation online.

Make your social media sites work for your personal web space

You can link back to your main website through any blogging, photo-sharing or social media sites that you belong to. These are valuable links to include but, as before, make sure that you are consistent in the use of your user name and choice of keywords across the sites, ensuring you have taken care to already clean up your digital spaces to show a consistent, professional profile – with personal images, comments, stories or videos either on a separate profile (not under your own name) or with privacy settings applied.

Free directories

As in the offline world, a *directory* is a site listing the names of other people or businesses. There are numerous directories available online, which might be willing to include a link to your website for free. Look for at least ten, and if you're really serious about building links, consider paying for some good quality listings as well.

As before, check the quality of the directories by using Google Page Rank, especially if you're paying for the link, since you only want links with those websites that have a page rank of one or above.

Linking don'ts

Minimise reciprocal links
If you have managed to secure some links from your friends' sites or other professional sites, try and avoid including a link back to their site, if possible. It might seem unfriendly, particularly with your friends, but reciprocal links cancel one another out so the advantage for your site will be lost. Instead, try and establish a round robin of links – this rates more favourably with the search engines.

Avoid link farms

These are pages full of links, which you'll no doubt discover from time to time when searching online. Link farms are spam – and viewed as such by Google – so a link farm containing your website will be of no value.

8.9 An example of a site containing links only

If you're unsure whether the site you're looking at is a link farm, as opposed to a directory, look for some common clues. Directories, for example, will often list a name and address as well as website URL. If you're still worried, avoid linking with any websites that include little or no text but ten or more links – usually a sure sign that it is a professional directory company to avoid.

TRICKS OF THE TRADE: USING PAID SEARCH

- When you search for a keyword on a search engine, you'll notice that in the results page two different types of results appear – unsponsored links in the main body of the page, and sponsored links, generally in the right column and also sometimes in the top few links on the results page.

Sponsored Links

Reputation Management
Manage your online reputation with the
Halpern Personal Reputation Management
book. Results Guaranteed
www.reputation-book.com

8.10 A sponsored (paid for) link

Personal Reputation Management Book
Personal Reputation Management can help you manage your online reputation so that you can be found by search engines, ...
www.reputation-book.com 11k - Cached - Similar pages

Personal Reputation Management Book - About the book
So too, it is becoming increasingly important for professionals, jobseekers, entrepreneurs and anyone else concerned with their **personal reputation** to take ...
www.reputation-book.com/about-the-book - 13k - Cached - Similar pages ilar pages

8.11 Non-sponsored (organic) links

- While the terminology may differ a little – Google uses 'sponsored links' for example, while Yahoo! prefers 'sponsor results' – the concept is the same across all search engines. The sponsored results are easily identifiable as they will be highlighted in a different colour or included in a separate column on the page.

- The tricks and techniques we've suggested in this book are designed to get your website recognised high up in the non-sponsored search listings. It is free to appear in these results and boosting your profile is down to the relevance and popularity of your site.

- However, if you're serious about getting your website noticed, you could consider paying for a sponsored link. This isn't difficult and doesn't have to be expensive You can also choose when to run the sponsored link, for example, in the 48 hours before or after you've been for a job interview, so that anyone searching for your name in a search engine will discover your website in the sponsored results.

- If you want your sponsored result to appear in Google you need to use Google AdWords (easily found by searching on Google). You can sign up to this online using the self-service function in a matter of minutes.

- The price you pay is determined by the number of people bidding on a keyword. For this reason, keyword phrases like 'car insurance' tend to be very expensive. But unless there are many people with your name, you're unlikely to find that your keyword costs much. In which case, the cost will come down to how often you want the ad to appear and where (in which regions, for example).

KEY LEARNINGS FROM THIS CHAPTER:

- This chapter is all about getting noticed by your target audience and the search engines. Decide on your plan of attack – whether that is being noticed on your social media sites or making your web space more visible – and remember that promoting your reputation is all about consistency, visibility and quality content repeated over time.

TOP TIPS FOR MAKING YOUR WEBSITE MORE VISIBLE:

■ Index your site on the three main search engines: Google, Yahoo! and Live Search (Microsoft's search engine).

■ Make sure that you fill in the page title of each page, as this is what search engines use first of all when searching your website.

■ Include your name at least once in the main copy on each page, but don't use it repeatedly in the hope that it will increase your position in search engine results. It won't, and search engines will instead regard your website as spam.

■ Don't include hidden links, as search engines will also view this as spam.

■ Don't use 'doorway pages' - web pages that contain several instances of a particular keyword to increase the site's ranking on a search engine – as you might find your site is 'blacklisted' by the search engines.

■ Building web links with other sites will help improve your ranking in search engine results, as the more popular your site, the more likely it is to rise to the top of a search engine's results page.

■ The higher a site's page ranking, the more valuable that link is to your website. To find out a site's page rank, simply download the Google toolbar (**www.toolbar.google.com**). You should be looking for sites with a page ranking of one or above.

■ Build links with friends' or colleagues' sites, but avoid including a link to their site, if possible, as reciprocal links cancel one another out.

■ Another way of building up quality links for your website is to comment on stories that are relevant to your website content. Also consider linking with associations, professional bodies, your employer or free directories.

TOP TIPS FOR USING SOCIAL MEDIA SITES TO MAKE YOU MORE VISIBLE:

■ Your personal reputation can live via any relevant social media tool as long as you follow some basic ground rules (see below).

■ Keep a consistent message across all your information online to maximise the reach of your brand.

■ Use each tool to tell your story in the best and most relevant way (eg. Twitter for regular updates and canvassing public opinion, a blog for more in-depth detail about your views, and so on).

■ Ensure you put your primary digital space contact details (your name, profession, phone and email address) on your CV, business documents, blog comments and others to maximise your online visibility.

■ Being visible is not as effective if you haven't defined your online framework: who you are and what your primary objective is (see chapter six to get started on this).

■ If you are new to social media networks have a look around first, and see if the types of people on those networks are allied to your profession, interests and common goals. Only join those that match your aspirations, otherwise you'll spend a lot of time cleaning up or managing your digital footprint on sites that aren't particularly useful to furthering your reputation online.

■ Remember that sites like Facebook use the same search engine as Live Search – so if you follow the same visibility rules you should appear high on both, although typically this takes longer than with your own website.

REPUTATION ACTION: HOW VISIBLE ARE YOUR MENTORS?

✔ Write down a list of the top five business or professional people you aspire to be like. They could be famous in the business world, like Richard Branson, or a global politician like Barack Obama. Alternatively, it might be someone in your industry you admire.

8.12   Richard Branson (Photograph taken by: Toby Barnes)

✔ Check if they are using the internet to spread their message and enhance their reputation through credibility, trust and a consistent telling of their story.

✔ Run through this checklist:

1. How many social networks do they appear on and why?

2. Do they have a web presence?

3. Are they using best practices in keeping the content on their site connected (page titles, headings, amount of content, links and so on)?

4. Do they have a personal blog? How often is it updated?

5. Are they using new technology like Twitter? If so, how many followers do they have?

6. How many people or sites are linking to them?

7. Is the content on their sites fresh, interesting and relevant?

8. How do you think that they are enhancing their own reputations as well as their company, brand or whatever they stand for through these online media?

✔ Some forward-thinking professionals will be applying some, if not all of these techniques but you'll probably discover that a large majority still aren't. With this in mind, work out how you could gain a competitive advantage through enhancing your visibility across your relevant online spaces.

Next chapter: How to maintain your online personal reputation

9

Maintaining your personal reputation

In this chapter, you will:

- Learn how to maintain your personal reputation
- Identify tools to help track your reputation across blogs, social media and the web
- Find out who is talking about you and how you can use this information to your advantage
- Learn techniques to minimise your time and maximise the effect on your reputation
- Know what to do if things go wrong

Don't stop now

You now understand the power of your reputation and how it can help you achieve your professional objectives. You've cleaned up your digital footprint on relevant social media networks, judiciously separated out your personal and professional life on Facebook, Flickr, LinkedIn and Twitter. You've decided what you want your online framework to be, and you understand what elements of your personal brand to maximise. A carefully built website is now live and is being indexed by all the major search engines. You might even have invested in a **PPC** *(See Pay Per Click)* campaign to boost your online profile after a job interview.

Thank heavens for that. That's your reputation sorted out once and for all, isn't it?

Well, we have good news... and bad news. The good news is you are now at the cutting edge of the new economy and you are presenting yourself as professional, knowledgeable about new technologies, and capable of showing initiative. Well done.

The bad news is that for your reputation to continue reaping benefits, you must nurture and care for it. The web isn't a static medium, like TV or print; it's constantly evolving and that means you need to be continually evolving with it.

Remember, protecting and promoting your reputation in the online sphere is as important as maintaining a respectable appearance or delivering work on time in the real world. This is your shop window, your battlefield. You are not going to let your hard work go to waste by failing to look after the one thing that could make the difference between you winning that new contract or being offered that shiny new job, are you?

This chapter is all about maintaining and monitoring your online reputation; don't forget you've done all the hard work already. This bit is going to be much easier now that you understand the power of your reputation and can begin utilising the inherent power of the internet to benefit it.

Monitoring your brand

People are talking about you right now. You are in the reputation business even if you don't know it. If you have a job or are actively searching for a job, trying to grow your business contacts or database, customers or potential employers could be weighing up whether to contact you or to pass right now.

You need to know who is talking about you, what they are saying about you and what to do about it.

There are a variety of reasons why your name may be mentioned on the internet – and not all of these mentions will necessarily be of benefit to you.

The good reasons

▪ Your name keeps on coming up when an employer searches on Facebook for 'freelance designers in London' because in all your social media profiles, tweets and blog comments you signed off with 'Joe Bloggs – London freelance designer, available for contracts'.

▪ Your new product or service is receiving great online PR from dedicated advocates due to you delivering a consistent message over time across several relevant social media sites.

▪ Your employer decided to check on all their employees to see who is helping or damaging the company image – and these days that could be the difference between company success and failure – to help decide whether you should be in the firing line when redundancies come around. On your LinkedIn homepage he sees your career mission statement and request for complementary professional contacts to help deliver an *R&D (See Research and Development)* project and decides you are a valuable asset to the company – others might not be so forward thinking.

The bad reasons

▪ A competitor is trying to discredit your service on an industry blog.

▪ A customer is fed up with perceived bad service from your company or brand and is telling everyone they know about it.

▪ A friend or colleague is maliciously spreading false rumours about you.

▪ A friend is uploading funny but inappropriate photographs or videos of you.

It's not all about Google

Until very recently an individual or company that wanted to utilise the internet to help monitor their brand had a very simple task. Have a quick check on Google and then you would be fully in control of everything being said about you on the internet. That is not the case any longer though. While Google still remains the dominant force in search engines, it is not the only one, and as we've seen earlier, search engines aren't the only places where you can be looked up.

Don't forget also, that the search engines don't know whether something being said about you is good or bad, legal or illegal. If there is relevant content spread across credible sources on the internet, the search engines will return it high in their results. However, even though the search engines are incredibly powerful tools, it is actually the people using them that make the difference. It is the people that matter, the people that you want to attract with your credible, professional reputation. These people will mind – they will mind a lot.

So the important thing to remember is that knowing who is talking about you is half the battle; understanding how to react to those conversations is the other half.

As we all know, the web is vast, and constantly growing, so trying to track where your name or website appears online isn't an easy task. Thankfully, there are some tools available to help. Even better, the ones we're suggesting you use are free.

The tools to find out who is talking about you.

Rather than typing your name into a search engine such as Google, Yahoo! or MSN every morning to see if anyone is talking about you online, there are a number of services that can do the job for you. If you understand that you or your brand might be talked about on blogs, social media networks, user-generated review sites or any other online spaces, you understand that knowing about them is crucial in responding, refuting and promoting your personal reputation.

Blogs

There are a number of free blog tracking tools, which let you know when someone is either talking about you or commenting on what you have said on another person or company's blog.

Technorati (www.technorati.com): This is the largest of the blog search engines. You simply register and then elect to receive RSS alerts any time the keywords you define are mentioned (a keyword could be your name or your company, for

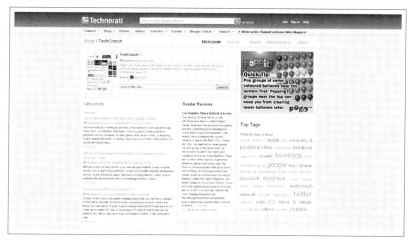

9.1 Blog search engine www.technorati.com

example.) You can also use this technology in a more proactive job hunting or lead producing manner.

Do it now: set up a Technorati RSS feed for the keywords covering your name, company, role, location, and salary. When non-traditionally advertised jobs are being discussed or commented on, or when employers or recruiters are looking for savvy, pro-active candidates, you can be at the head of the queue. Similarly, as a business person you can subscribe to RSS feeds based around typical complaints in your industry (i.e. shoddy work, does anyone know a good plumber etc...)

Reacting and responding to these types of conversations is an excellent way to develop honest and credible relationships and to quickly enhance your personal reputation. With continued monitoring and maintenance of your reputation in this way it soon becomes clear to your target audience that you are efficient, forward thinking, and are someone they would want to do business with.

Backtype (www.backtype.com): This tool allows you to monitor who is mentioning you in various blog post comments. This means that you can track across the whole blogosphere very easily. It also allows you to track your own comments on various industry, professional or service blogs – and you have the ability to include a web link back to your own blog or website. What's effective about this approach is that if you are joining in your industry's social media or blog conversations (and you really should be – if you don't know where to start, type 'your industry forums' or 'your industry community' into Google) across the internet, people can find you if they are interested in what you have to say on your blog comments – this could be as simple as you always signing off your blog comments with a professional status update:

"Joe Bloggs – Freelance interior designer, available from May 8 for work. See my web space, LinkedIn profile or follow me on Twitter here."

Social media tools

Social Mention (www.socialmention.com): This social media aggregation tool allows you to see what is being said about you or your business on all of your social media spaces such as LinkedIn, Facebook, Flickr, Twitter, and many others. It also offers the ability to narrow down your search to blogs, microblogs, images, news or comments – or alternatively to search for them all at once.

FriendFeed (www.friendfeed.com): Use this tool to find out what is being said about you on social media sites. Sign up for a free account and then connect all of your existing Facebook, Flickr accounts etc.

9.2   www.friendfeed.com - a social network content aggregator

Twitter (http://twitter.com): In addition to using Twitter to manage and monitor your tweets, retweets and replies to tweets, there are a number of Twitter tools available to monitor and track all Twitter references to you online. For example, you can track how many times one of your tweets has been retweeted down the line. Ensure you set up RSS feeds to wherever you would like to receive your information – as with all the other social media, web and blog tools. Alternatively use a monitoring service such as **www.monitter. com** to aggregate your Twitter results in real time. This is particularly useful if you have a mature online profile and brand.

Web tools - Google Alerts (www.google.com/alerts)

Google Alerts

Manage your Alerts

Your Google Alerts

Search terms	Type
☐ celebrity gossip	Video
☐ Joe Bloggs	Comprehensive
☐ personal reputation	Comprehensive
☐ technology	News
☐ web trends	News

[Delete]

9.3 Receive email updates for your search terms with Google alerts

Google Alerts are email updates of the latest relevant Google results (from the web, news, blogs and so on) based on your choice of query or topic. So if you want to hear about 'business opportunities in London' for example, you could set up a Google Alert to receive updates on that phrase whenever it appears on Google.

More importantly in this case, you should set up a Google Alert for yourself e.g. 'Joe Bloggs' (not 'Joe' or 'Bloggs' on their own, as you'll receive far too many unnecessary responses). Simply visit **www.google.com/alerts** and in the 'create a Google Alert' box insert the search term you want to follow.

Choose the type of information you want to track. We'd suggest using 'comprehensive' rather than a specific category like 'news' as you want to find out what's being said about you across as many sites and web spaces as possible. Then choose how often you wish to receive the alerts – you might want to start with 'as it happens', so you receive an alert whenever your name is mentioned online – but you can change this if it becomes a burden to manage. Finally, submit your email address, as you'll be receiving the alerts via email.

You can create as many Google Alerts as you want and manage them by signing in with your Google ID (you will have created this already if using any Google applications like Blogger). Simply follow the link at the bottom of the email alert.

Be aware that Google Alerts won't provide you with 100 per cent coverage of what's being said about you online – it doesn't monitor all news sources, for example. So make sure that you dedicate some time each month to typing your name into different search engines and seeing what features in the results, and how this changes over time.

You could also use Yahoo Pipes (**http://pipes.yahoo.com**), which offers a similar free service to Google Alerts.

THIS SOUNDS FINE FOR PEOPLE WHO WORK IN THE DIGITAL SPHERE BUT WHAT ABOUT ME, I'M A BUILDER?

+ Your customers are finding you through a variety of different means both online and offline – this may include recommendations, customer testimonies, online listings, or traditional means such as local newspaper listings or the Yellow Pages. By utilising some of the easy to implement monitoring techniques we're suggesting online, you can get ahead of your competitors and use the internet to help maintain and grow your business. Your reputation is about what you offer professionally as a person and a business, so why not take advantage of an ever-expanding, cheap and effective means of getting your message out there?

Google Reader (reader.google.com)

Setting up a Google Reader to aggregate all of the things being said about you and your brand online is another good approach. This allows you to manage all the conversations through blogs, Twitter, social networks and other online spaces in one place.

9.4 Use Google reader to keep up with blogs and news

Free tools or paid services?

If you are just starting out in managing your online reputation, the free tools that are available online will suffice perfectly well. If you are an individual who has a larger brand presence – for instance a mature LinkedIn profile, a web space, a blog, and a long-standing online presence – one of the paid services might be more in keeping with your level of requirement. To find one, simply type 'reputation management' or 'personal reputation management' into Google to get some more ideas.

Of course, you may also want to keep a track of the things people are saying about your company, your CEO or managing director, so you can be prepared with a proactive plan if you or your company's reputation is attacked online. You could also extend this to seeing what is being said about your competitors, whether they be individuals or businesses. Just be mindful that looking after your own reputation should always come first. Understand that what people are saying about your direct competitors is valuable in terms of visibility across the larger landscape, but not anywhere near as effective as promoting and protecting your own reputation.

Now I know what's being said about me on the internet, how do I respond or use it to my advantage?

Being in control of the facts is half the battle; if you don't know what is being said, you can't plan how to maximise the good things and minimise the bad things. It's also good to know if nothing is being said about you, as this is something else you can address easily using some of our suggested techniques.

Now that you know what is being said about you online – whether someone is criticising your personal reputation, your competitors are trying to undermine your authority or recruiters in your sector are actively seeking candidates – you can do something about it. Start a conversation, apply for a job or offer to better the deal your customer has been given by a competitor – whatever is relevant to your circumstances at that time. Be proactive in your communications, let people know you exist, what you have to offer and be steadfast in always maintaining a professional reputation online, and you will see results quickly.

Say what you want to say but do it wisely

Consistency is the key to promoting your online reputation successfully. Regardless of whether you are just beginning to improve your online reputation, taking steps to monitor and make smaller changes to your online profile, or even if you are responding to false information that has been posted about you or your company, the same rules apply.

A measured and considered approach works best online. It is very easy to bash out an angry response to a customer or potential employer, or to publicise bad practice by your competitors. But one of the dangers of instantaneously being able to connect to millions of potential people is that once you have hit 'send' or posted a comment, you can't take it back. So remember: what you say and how you say it are vitally important in building and maintaining a positive online profile.

Trip Advisor, eBay and Amazon are all examples of sites that promote user-generated content to help other people make buying decisions. If you were conducting an eBay auction and received a bid for a large item you would most likely check out the person's profile to ensure they were a credible bidder. And if their profile contained several bad reviews, you'd be more likely not to accept the bid. So even in a basic way, a person's online reputation can be tarnished simply through their eBay actions.

As time goes by, it's not just the internet that will evolve; inevitably your circumstances will change too, so you need to be continually updating the framework of your online profile – be that through your website or membership of several social media sites – to reflect these developments.

The changes might be minor, but make sure to include them. For example, you'll have another year's experience in the industry, you might have delivered a project that demonstrates a new area of expertise, or you might have landed your first job after graduating and need to update your CV to reflect your new circumstances.

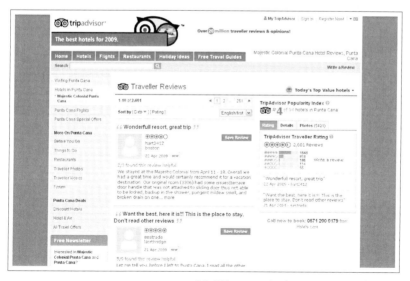

9.5 Write your own travel reviews on www.tripadvisor.com

Whatever your situation, make sure that you review and update your content every three months; this will also help ensure that the search engines continue to index your profiles.

Back to Google - maintaining your search engine ranking

Search engines are also constantly developing their technology to improve the accuracy and relevancy of search engine results for users. For this reason, they often change their algorithms – the way they measure and rank websites to match keywords – to improve the user's search experience.

Consequently, you need to monitor your search engine ranking and ensure that it either maintains or increases its position over time.

Bear in mind that during the first three months your search engine ranking probably won't increase drastically – despite following everything we've suggested in the previous chapter. This isn't because the techniques don't work; rather, it's due to the way search engines work and the fact that they take time to notice changes to websites and update their systems.

So it's a good idea to track your position closely. This way you'll notice any changes in your search engine listing over time. We suggest creating a simple Excel spreadsheet and logging your position as often as you can manage it (ideally, once a week).

If you followed the suggestions we made in previous chapters, you should see your ranking increase over time. If it doesn't, it could be due to a number of reasons. The worst-case scenario is that it falls significantly as a result of your site being blacklisted and falling foul of a search engine's guidelines.

But if you've followed the best practices we've outlined, it's unlikely that you'll see such a drop in traffic. Instead, a dip in your position is more likely to be due to a quality link disappearing (the networking group you signed up to might have ceased, for example) or perhaps someone with the same or a similar name to you has increased their search engine ranking to your detriment.

Don't panic, though. As in the real world, when a competitive threat emerges you simply need to go through the best reputation practices that we have highlighted.

For instance, aim to rewrite at least 10 to 15 per cent of your website copy every three months. If you don't feel you have anything new to add, just rearrange the order of sentences or rephrase some of the copy without losing your main keywords. Search engines will register that as a change and it will have an impact on your ranking as a result.

Also, continue to build as many high quality links with your site as possible. This is an ongoing task – perhaps consider it as another form of networking – so whenever you meet someone or an organisation that's complementary to your job or profession, ask if you can have a link on their site. And keep an eye on any new free directories that emerge, as they're always a good source of quality links.

Finally, if you're contacted through your website, ask that person or organisation how they found you. It's standard practice in the business world to ask customers where they found out about a product or service but somehow when it comes to our own reputation, we seem to forget to do the same. But by finding out how someone found you, you'll know which are the high quality links to your site or how effective your search engine ranking is in delivering new business to you.

Q. What to do if you find negative comments

Answer: If someone is deliberately trying to sabotage your chances of gaining employment (or your business if you're self-employed), there are ways of tackling the situation professionally, without resorting to a counter smear campaign.

For a start, if you're managing your personal reputation effectively, you'll already have made sure that your website and the other positive things you want people to read about you (perhaps through your LinkedIn profile, Flickr page and so on) rank highly in the search engines whenever anyone searches on your name. If you've followed the practices we suggested, your site and other sites linked to you should appear higher in the search engine results than any negative comments made online by someone else.

Now, onto the thornier subject of tackling the negative press. Start by contacting the person making the allegations and asking them to remove them if they are clearly lies. Perhaps it's a friend playing a joke or trying to cause you some discomfort. In this case, they'll probably remove the content if you ask them to, especially if they feel embarrassed by their behaviour.

If this doesn't work, the threat of legal action may help. In the majority of cases, this will solve the problem as most people are intimidated by the possibility of legal proceedings.

However, if this doesn't have the desired effect, you can start legal proceedings against them if they are saying defamatory things about you. Libellous comments made on the web are taken just as seriously by the courts as comments made in a newspaper or broadcast on air, so you will have somewhere to find redress. However, be aware that any legal action will involve costs.

If you're unsure of how to proceed, contact the Citizens Advice Bureau, who will be able to tell you exactly what your rights are and where to find help. Remember, your reputation is your livelihood so it's important that you take every step possible to protect it.

KEY LEARNINGS FROM THIS CHAPTER

■ Managing your personal reputation online should be an ongoing task – not only because the web is a constantly evolving medium, but also because your brand will change over time too.

■ Set up Google Alerts – it will only take you 10 minutes and covers a huge amount of the content available on the web.

■ Pick a frequency and time to monitor your online reputation and try and stick to it. Organise several RSS feeds into your Google Reader from the web, Facebook, Twitter, LinkedIn and the blogosphere. This will give you a good overview of what is being said about you and your brand. To begin with, do this once a week until you have built up enough conversations, comments and people who are interested in what you have to say, then once your reputation matures a little you should see recruiters, employers or business contacts starting to contact you about relevant matters – and your aim should be to develop these relationships into job offers or business opportunities.

■ Monitoring your brand is not just about knowing when someone is saying something about you, it is about having effective strategies in place to deal with both positive and negative feedback. This could be anything from replying to an informal Twitter from a recruitment company wanting to know about your employment status, to a more formal response to a request for tender from a client who has seen your name mentioned several times in a positive way and wants you to pitch for a piece of new business. Each approach requires a different mindset, although the objective should always be the same – to continue the dialogue further and for that dialogue to be mutually beneficial.

- Continually update your 'online CV' – be that through your website or membership of different social media sites – to reflect changes to your personal circumstances, however minor (so even if it's that you've worked in the industry for an extra year, update your information to say this).

- Monitor your search engine rankings every week using a simple Excel spreadsheet.

- Aim to rewrite at least 10 to 15 per cent of the copy on your website every three months.

- Continue to build as many high quality links with your site as possible and keep an eye on any new free directories that emerge, as they're always a good source of quality links.

- If you're contacted through your website, ask that person or organisation how they found you, so you know which links are valuable to you or how effective your search engine ranking is in delivering new business.

REPUTATION ACTION: COMPETITOR REVIEW

✔ Choose a couple of your competitors – they could be individuals from other companies, students in your final year degree class or other companies. Set up a quick Google Alert and monitor it twice a week for 10 minutes.

- Did your competitors get mentioned very often?

- If so was it all positive or were there some negative comments?

- Did you see any comments or replies from your competitors to any negative or positive press?

- Could they have handled it better?

- Were they calm, courteous and professional in their dealings with customers or employers?

NEGATIVE WEBSITE REVIEW

✔ Now find one or two negative websites - If you conduct a search engine query for 'bad customer service' you should find something quite easily. There are also several famous cases involving multinational food, technology and service companies that you could look at.

✔ The aim of this exercise is to review these companies and cases and see how they dealt with complaints and negative reviews. Keep these strategies in mind in case you need to use them further down the track.

SITES THAT COUNTERACT NEGATIVE PRESS

✔ Find one or two people or companies who have set up websites to counteract negative press – search under

REPUTATION ACTION: COMPETITOR REVIEW (CONT.)

'bad PR' or 'PR and companies' as there are quite a few cases where people and companies have taken extreme measures to protect their reputations.

✔ Think about:

- Who came out ahead with a stronger reputation or more loyal customers than before the event?

- Who buried their heads in the sand and downgraded their own reputation in the process?

- Did anyone try to bully individuals or become overly aggressive?

✔ Now try the same exercise with individuals. To get you started type 'internet defamation' into your search engine and have a look at the top few results. Consider the same questions above.

✔ These exercises will give you a taste of how powerful reputation is for individuals and companies. At the extreme end it can mean the difference between an individual's successful career or not, or a company going out of business or thriving.

✔ Look at the positive and negative in these examples, and utilise only the best case studies in managing your online reputation – it will reap dividends.

Now it is up to you

Congratulations!
You are now well positioned at the forefront of the reputation revolution. As the information century unfolds and digital touchpoints become more and

more prevalent in all our daily lives, you can harness them more effectively. Protect and promote your reputation, put your best foot forward and show your audience what you are made of. The world is watching, online reputation management is the key.

Now that we're at the end of the book, we hope you have a better understanding of how powerful your reputation is and what it can do for your professional and personal objectives. When all is said and done the key difference is you.

Please take away these key messages to get started on your personal reputation management journey. Good luck!

- Those who look after their reputation will see the benefits increase exponentially.

- You have gained a competitive advantage by even beginning to think about your reputation this much.

- You don't have to be technical to understand and deliver on your online reputation.

- It is a quick and simple task to maintain and monitor your reputation online.

- Your reputation matters, look after it.

References

Chapter 1: Introduction

i. http://www.politics.co.uk/opinion-formers/British-Security-Industry-Association/
about-the-UK-security-industry-$365890$2.htmhttp://startupmeme.com/facebook-
reaches-120-million-users-worldwide/

ii. http://www.techcrunch.com/2008/11/03/three-billion-photos-at-flickr/

iii. http://www.accuracast.com/search-daily-news/seo-7471/first-page-listings-on-
google-even-more-important/

iv. The Times, 19 April 2007

v. Daily Mail, 20 November, page 7

vi. www.google.co.uk

vii. www.leeds.ac.uk/media/news/hill.htm

viii. www.telegraph.co.uk/news/uknews/3484612/Rod-Lucas-dropped-by-TalkSPORT-
after-BNP-links-emerge.html

ix. www.rodlucas.com

x. www.alexa.com

xi. www.alexa.com

xii. news.bbc.co.uk/2/hi/business/6034577.stm

Chapter 2: A brief history of reputation

i. Ian Tattershall, 'once we were not alone', Scientific American, January 2000, p. 43

ii. http://www.sirc.org/publik/belonging.pdf

iii. Wood, Francis (2002). The Silk Road: Two Thousand Years in the Heart of Asia Berkeley, CA: University of California Press. pp. 9, 13–23. ISBN 978-0-520-24340-8

iv. A Short History of the World, HG Wells, 1922, Penguin Modern Classics

v. A Scandalous history of the Roman Emperors, Anthony Blond, Robinson, 1994

vi. www.dailymail.co.uk/news/article-1066425/Arise-Lord-Sleaze-Brown-resurrects-Peter-Mandelson---disgraced-Prince-Darkness

vii. http://en.wikipedia.org/wiki/Neuro-linguistic_programming

viii. www.dangers-of-hypnosis.co.uk/hypnosis_another_perception.html

ix. http://www.chrismorris.com/about-chris.html

Chapter 3: Everyone's famous now

i. http://www.magforum.com

ii. http://www.mediatel.co.uk

iii. http://news.bbc.co.uk/1/hi/uk/3007871.stm

iv. http://en.wikipedia.org/wiki/Pete_Townshend#Legal_matters

v. http://news.bbc.co.uk/1/hi/uk/3007871.stm

vi. http://news.bbc.co.uk/1/hi/uk/3007871.stm

vii. http://www.newsoftheworld.co.uk/showbiz/xfactor/article93748.ece

viii. http://dontdatehimgirl.com/faqs/

ix. http://www.shinyshiny.tv/2007/08/weird_website_o.html

x. http://www.cfinst.org/pr/prRelease.aspx?ReleaseID=155

xi. http://www.democraticunderground.com/discuss/duboard.php?az=view_all&address=132x5990249

xii. http://blogs.wsj.com/biztech/2008/03/03/internet-lessons-from-nine-inch-nails-and-obama/

Chapter 4: The law and your reputation

i. http://en.wikipedia.org/wiki/Section_230_of_the_Communications_Decency_Act

ii. http://www.theregister.co.uk/2006/07/03/dontdatehim_sued/

iii. http://www.citmedialaw.org/threats/hollis-v-cunningham

iv. http://www.theregister.co.uk/2008/11/03/chinese_official_sacked/

v. http://uk.reuters.com/article/technologyNews/idUKTRE4A22NN20081103
vi. http://chinadigitaltimes.net/2008/11/lin-jiaxiang-sacked-but-cleared-of-molestation-charges/
vii. http://news.xinhuanet.com/english/2008-11/06/content_10313508.htm
viii. http://www.ironport.com/company/pp_reuters_12-03-2007.html
ix. http://security.tekrati.com/research/10059/
x. http://www.guardian.co.uk/money/2006/feb/02/idcards.business
xi. http://www.denisatlas.co.uk/

Chapter 5: Social media

i. http://www.brandrepublic.com/News/788606/YouTube-replaces-Wikipedia-popular-social-media-site
ii. http://www.alexa.com/site/ds/top_sites?cc=US&ts_mode=country&lang=none
iii. www.techcrunch.com/2008/06/12/facebook-no-longer-the-second-largest-social-network
iv. www.social-media-optimization.com/2008/03/top-10-video-sites
v. Choi, J. H. (2006). Living in Cyworld: Contextualising Cy-Ties in South Korea. In A. Bruns & J. Jacobs (Eds.), Use of Blogs (Digital Formations) (pp. 173-186). New York: Peter Lang
vi. www.alexa.com
vii. http://www.comscore.com/press/release.asp?press=2051

Chapter 6: Defining yourself online

i. http://www.nielsen-online.com/pr/pr_081125.pdf
ii. http://www.nielsen-online.com/pr/pr_080214_UK.pdf
iii. http://www.statistics.gov.uk/cci/nugget.asp?id=12
iv. http://news.bbc.co.uk/1/hi/uk/7802461.stm
v. http://weblogs.hitwise.com/robin-goad/2008/12/facebook_youtube_christmas_social_networking.html

Chapter 7: Tools and technology

i.   http://news.bbc.co.uk/1/hi/technology/7671718.stm
ii. http://www.comscore.com/press/release.asp?press=2616
iii. http://en.wikipedia.org/wiki/Wikipedia:About
iv. http://en.wikipedia.org/wiki/Wikipedia:About
v.   http://en.wikipedia.org/wiki/Knol
vi. http://www.id-protect.co.uk/news.php?news_id=739

Chapter 8: Getting people, search engines and social networks to notice you

i.   (not including mapping, local directory, and user-generated video searches) Nielsen Online Search Share Rankings, ratings October 2008
ii. http://news.bbc.co.uk/1/hi/technology/4685750.stm
iii. http://en.thinkexist.com/quotation/it_takes_many_good_deeds_to_build_a_good/184532.html
iv. http://weblogs.hitwise.com/robin-goad/2008/02/google_blacklists_gocompare.html

Image Credits

Chapter 1: Introduction

1.1
page 16

Imitation of the Google homepage with "You" entered into the search box.

1.2
page 18

First: Happy to be skiing. Uploaded to stock.xchng (**www.sxc.hu**) by Ned Horton using the profile *hortongrou*.
Second: Green boy. Uploaded to stock.xchng (**www.sxc.hu**) by Dani Alvarez using the profile *altrans*.

1.3
page 19

Photograph of headline in a local newspaper. Uploaded to stock.xchng (**www.sxc.hu**) by Dez Pain using the profile *xymonau*.

1.4
page 21

Selection of mobile devices
Blackberry Mobile. Uploaded to Flickr (**www.flickr.com**) by *StrebKR*.
Apple Macbook Pro. Uploaded to Flickr (**www.flickr.com**) by *geerlingguy*.
Apple iPhone. Uploaded to Flickr (**www.flickr.com**) by Terry Johnston using the profile *powerbooktrance*.

1.5
page 30

Screenshot of the first page of Google's search results for the search "Reverend John Stanton".

1.6
page 30

Screenshot of the first page of Google's search results for the search "Rod Lucas".

1.7
page 33

Collection of logos of the major search engines.

1.8   Screenshot of the YouTube homepage - **www.youtube.com**
page 34

1.9   Modified screenshot of the first page of Google's search results for the
page 36   search "Joe Bloggs".

Chapter 2: A brief history of reputation

2.1   Photograph of a cave painting in Sahara, Algeria.
page 40   Photographed and uploaded to Flickr (**www.flickr.com**) by Patrick
          Gruban using the profile *Gruban*.

2.2   Scanned image of early wine merchants from an unknown source. Scanned
page 44   and uploaded to **www.pbm.com/~lindahl/food-art** by Cindy Renfrow.

2.3   *Anthony & Cleopatra*, painted by Lawrence Alma-Tadema (1885, Oil on
page 45   panel. 65.5 x 92 cm). Source: Wikipedia (**en.wikipedia.org**).

2.4   Engraving of printer using the early Gutenberg letter press during the 15th
page 46   century. Source: Wikipedia (**en.wikipedia.org**).

2.5   Modified reprint of The London Gazette front page from Monday 3 - 10
page 47   September 1666, reporting on the Fire of London. Source: Wikipedia (**en.
          wikipedia.org**).

2.6   Photograph of Peter Mandelson at the Hearings of the Commissioners-
page 52   designate, European Parliament in 2004. Source: **www.europarl.europa.eu**

Chapter 3: Everyone's famous now

3.1   Pete Townshend playing the guitar at a The Who concert at the Verizon
page 57   Center in Washington, D.C., USA. Photographed by Ian MacIsaac, March
          9th, 2007. Source: Wikipedia (**en.wikipedia.org**).

3.2   The X Factor, American Idol and Britian's Got Talent logos
page 58

3.3   Screenshot of the dontdatehimgirl homepage - **www.dontdatehimgirl.com**
page 60

3.4   Screenshot of the the Drudge Report homepage - **www.drudgereport.com**
page 61

3.5   Official presidential portrait of Barack Obama, taken shortly before he
page 62   assumed office. Photographed by Pete Souza, The Obama-Biden Transition
           Project. Source: Change.gov (**change.gov**).

3.6   Screenshot of President Barack Obama's Twitter page - **www.twitter.**
page 63   **com/BarackObama**

Chapter 4: The law and your reputation

4.1   Screenshot of the first page of Google's search results for the search "Colin
page 70   Montgomerie speeding".

4.2   Screen shot of the video clip footage allegedly showing Lin Jiaxiang taking
page 71   a young girl to the restrooms. Uploaded to YouTube by *stmon99*.

4.3   Screenshot of the Tom Cruise homepage - **www.tomcruise.com**
page 72

4.4   Screenshot of the Tom Cruise Nuts homepage - **www.tomcruisenuts.com**
page 72

Chapter 5: Social media

5.1   Collection of logos for the leading brands related with social media.
page 78

5.2   Diagram.
page 80

Chapter 6: Defining yourself online

6.1   Diagram.

page 90

6.2   Simple website design.

page 94

6.3   Homepage screenshot for a fictional website - **www.joebloggs.com**

page 101

Chapter 7: Tools & technology

7.1   Collection of the distribution tool logos available.

page 115

7.2   Collection of the distribution tool logos available

page 128

7.3   *Top:* Screenshot of the set-up screen for creating a new blog on Blogger -

page 131   **www.blogger.com**
             Bottom-Left: Screenshot of the Wordpress homepage - **www.wordpress.com**
             Bottom-Right: Screenshot of the Typepad homepage - **www.typepad.com**

7.4   Screenshot of the commenting box on Louis Halpern's View -

page 133   **www.louishalpern.com**

7.5   Homepage screenshot of Roy Murphy's personal website -

page 134   **www.roymurphy.com**

7.6   Screenshot of the first page of Google's search results for the search "John

page 136   Smith".

7.7   Homepage screenshots of various domain name registrars.

page 139   *Top-Left:* 123-reg - **www.123-reg.co.uk**
             Top-Right: Easily - **www.easily.co.uk**
             Bottom-Left: 1&1 - **www.1and1.co.uk**
             Bottom-Right: Nominet - **www.nominet.co.uk**

7.8   Screenshot of Joe Blogg's homepage
page 144

Chapter 8: Getting the search engines and your audience to notice you

8.1   Screenshot of the Google add URL website -
page 156   **www.google.co.uk/addurl/?continue=/addurl**

8.2   Screenshots of the browser title bars for the BBC
page 158   *Top:* BBC homepage - **www.bbc.co.uk**
             Bottom: BBC News page - **news.bbc.co.uk**

8.3   Screenshots of browser title bars for other big brand websites
page 158   *Top:* Apple Store UK - **store.apple.com/uk-store**
             Middle: Times Online - **www.timesonline.co.uk**
             Bottom: Sainsbury's - **www.sainsburys.co.uk**

8.4   Diagram
page 164

8.5   Screenshot of the Google Toolbar add-on at the top of a browser.
page 165

8.6   Created example of a public profile on Facebook - **www.facebook.com**
page 169

8.7   Created example of a public profile on LinkedIn - **www.linkedin.com**
page 170

8.8   Created example of a public profile on Twitter - **www.twitter.com**
page 170

8.9   Screenshot of a directory listing page - **directory.seo-supreme.com**
page 173

8.10   Screenshot of an example of a sponsored or paid for link on a Google
page 174   search results page.

8.11   Screenshot of an example of a non-sponsored or organic link on a Google
page 174   search results page.

8.12   Photograph of Richard Branson, CEO of Virgin. Photographed and
page 178   uploaded by Toby Barnes as *tobybarnes*.

Chapter 9: Maintaining your personal reputation

9.1   Homepage screenshot of Technorati, the blog search engine -
page 185   **www.technorati.com**

9.2   Screenshot of an example RSS feed page on Friend Feed - **www.friendfeed.com**
page 186

9.3   Screenshot example of a Google alerts list associated with certain requests
page 187   - **www.google.com/alerts**

9.4   Screenshot example of a user's Google Reader list - **reader.google.com**
page 189

9.5   Screenshot of a review on TripAdvisor created by a registered user -
page 191   **www.tripadvisor.com**

Glossary

A

Algorithm

The logic that a search engine uses to decide whether a website is relevant to the term a user has typed into a search input box

Alt Tag

A description added to online images to ensure that search engines are able to recognise the content contained with each image.

B

Backlinks

(Also known as 'Inbound links') Incoming links to a webpage or website host.

Beta

A digital project which has passed the first stage of development testing and has been handed over to users for software testing. The objective feedback from users enables developers to identify issues that may have been overlooked in the first phase of testing.

Blacklisted	A penalty for websites that do not adhere to a search engine's code of best practice. The offending site is removed from the search engine list for a period of time and will not appear in search results.
Blog, Blogging	A blog is a small website containing content which is generally written by a single user. Blogs aim to provide up-to-date information, viewpoints of the author or commentary about a particular subject or theme.
Blogosphere	Used to describe the large and influential network of blogs that make up the blogging community on the internet.
Brand	An identity that a person, company or product assumes in order to be recognisable to consumers and differentiate itself from competitors.
Brand values	The core attributes that direct all marketing activity, packaging and interaction a brand has with their consumers. E.g. Virgin's brand values are value for money, quality, innovation, fun and a sense of competitive challenge.
Browser	A program used to view or interact with content on the World Wide Web. E.g. Internet Explorer or Mozilla Firefox.

C

Content Management System	(abbrev. CMS) An online system that allows users with little or no knowledge of web coding to make changes to a website.
Copy	The textual content that appears on websites. Copy can be written for the purpose of informing or influencing the reader. Good copy must connect with and engage the audience.

D

Directory
A list of websites organised by category. E.g. Yahoo! or the Open Directory Project.

Domain name
An identification label used for addressing purposes on the internet. Most common are Top-Level-Domains (TLDs) which function as website addresses (i.e. http://www.example.net). They are usually set up as http://www.name.domain. Most common TLDs are .com, .org, .net, with some TLDs reserved for government institutions.

F

Forums
Online bulletin boards used for holding discussions and posting user generated content. E.g. **www.webdesignerforum.co.uk** is a forum where web designers can discuss new ideas, media campaigns or get feedback on their work.

G

Googling
The act of searching for something or someone using a search engine

H

HTML Coding
(Hyper Text Markup Language) A programming code used by web developers to describe different attributes on a web page and provide instructions on how the information contained within the page should be displayed.

Hosting
A service that runs servers connected to the internet, allowing organisations and individuals to serve content online. The most common kind

of hosting is web hosting which provides space on servers and connectivity to the internet for websites and databases.

I

Identity theft

The use of personal details such as bank details, address or confidential details to commit fraudulent actions.

Internet Service Provider

(abbrev. ISP) A company that provides users with access to the internet via broadband or dial up connection. E.g. AOL or BT Internet.

K

Keywords

A significant word or phrase used to describe the content on a webpage. Web users can search for relevant information by typing a keyword or phrase into a search engine. E.g. a recent graduate looking for a job might use keywords such as 'graduate recruitment', 'internship'.

Knol

A project started by Google that aims to collect user-generated articles about a variety of different topics. The term knol refers to the project as a whole and a single article within the website. The Knol website address is **knoll.google.com**.

L

Link Building

A process that creates inbound links to a website. This can be done by negotiating reciprocal links (see 'Inbound Reciprocal links'), or by arranging for the website to be listed in e-zines, newsletters, directories or search engines.

O

Offering

A product, piece of information or service that is presented to a website visitor (e.g. accountancy services).

Online community

A group of people who are members of a website or have shared interests or lifestyles. E.g. i-genius. org is a website that offers entrepreneurs an online space where they can connect with other entrepreneurs, find out about networking events in their area and discuss topics of interest to them and their business.

Organic Search Results

Refers to the 'natural' or unpaid listings in search engines. The higher a site appears on these listings, the more traffic it can expect to attract.

M

Microblogging

A multi-media form of blogging that allows users to post pictures, video or short pieces of text onto a website. A micro-blog generally has the same purpose as a blog but the amount of content posted at one time is much smaller. Examples of micro-blogging sites include Twitter, Friendfeed and Plurk.

N

Neuro-Linguistic Programming

(abbrev. NLP) A technique that aims to change the unconscious thought process in order to alter participants' psychological responses to situations. NLP practitioners believe that this will enable them to communicate more effectively and overcome behavioural traits or habits that may limit performance in order to achieve excellence in a chosen field.

P

Page Title

The page title appears at the top of a web browser and is used to describe the content on the page being viewed. The text within the page title is used by search engines in order to create a page ranking.

Page Ranking

A number between 1 and 10 that represents how important Google considers a web page to be (1 denotes a low value, 10 is high). This is based on the number of links to and from a website, the importance of the parties who link to a particular web page and the relevance of items on that page. Pages with good page rankings will appear higher in organic or natural search results generated by Google.

Pay Per Click (PPC)

(abbrev. PPC) A model of advertising that allows companies to pay to ensure they appear when search engine results that are relevant to their website are displayed. Instead of paying every time an advert is displayed, a company will only pay each time an advert is clicked on by a web user.

R

Research and Development

(abbrev. R&D) The creative processes during which new ideas, practises and products are explored and assessed for commercial or practical value.

Registrar

An organization or service that offers management and reservation of Internet Domain Names (i.e. http://www.example.net) in accordance with the guidelines of the designated domain name registries to the public.

Reciprocal links

A process where the owners of two separate websites agree to create a link to each others websites in order to improve their page ranking.

RSS feed	A list of frequently updated data such as news articles, blog entries, financial reports or podcasts that web users can subscribe to. An RSS feed will include a summary of the text as well as information on authorship or publishing dates. Web users who have subscribed to a particular feed will be able to see when it is updated using an RSS reader.
RSS reader	A tool that allows users to read any RSS feeds that they have subscribed to. The RSS reader will display the most up to date version of each feed and may also highlight which updates have not yet been read.

S

Search engine	A web search engine looks for information stored on the World Wide Web. This information could be contained in web pages, online videos, forums or blogs. The most famous example of a search engine would be Google but there are many other versions of search engines. E.g. Yahoo search or, more recently, Wolfram Alpha, Bing or Twittersearch.
Search engine indexing	The process whereby a search engine creates a list of websites and relevant keywords that it can reference when a web user does a search. This makes it quicker for the search engine to return relevant websites than if it had to search everything on the internet every time it was used.
Search engine results	The content that is displayed by a search engine after a user has searched for information.
Search engine optimisation	(abbrev. SEO) The process of improving a website so that it gets a higher volume or better quality of traffic. A well optimised website will appear higher on search results generated by a search engine
Search ranking	The position at which a website appears within the list of search results returned for

a particular keyword.

Site indexing A process that places a website onto a search engine so that it will appear in the results generated by relevant search terms.

Social bookmarking A method for web users to store and share lists of websites that they feel are interesting or topical. Social bookingmarking sites encourage users to use tags to describe each bookmark rather using than a formalised filing structure. The sites allow users to search for content using tags and will display information such as tags and number of bookmarks along with each piece of content. Examples of sites include Digg.com, StumbleUpon.com and Technorati.com.

Social media An umbrella term to describe the tools and online spaces where users can post text, video and pictures. Blogs are widely used social media tools as are social media websites such as Facebook or Twitter.

Social network A web of people connected by interests, location or lifestyle e.g. Facebook or MySpace. The people within a social network will use it to post user-generated content or commentary and to connect with and meet other people.

Spam Unwanted and unsolicited messages sent to a user on the internet. The most commonly experienced type is email spam, although it can appear on online forums or web-based forms.

T

Tag A descriptive word applied to a page or piece of content that allows it to be found easily by users or search engines.

U

Unique selling point

(abbrev. USPs) The feature or benefit that makes you, your product or service different to that provided by a competitor. USPs can either be factual (e.g. A particular lawyer has won more awards than any other professional within their field), or emotional (e.g. this brand of makeup will make you feel as glamorous as a particular film star.)

Uniform Resource Locator

(abbrev. URL) The address of where a website or file is stored on the World Wide Web e.g. the URL of the Halpern Cowan website is www. halperncowan.com.

User generated content

Text, images or video created by individuals in a personal capacity. For example YouTube or Tripadvisor.

V

Virtual reality

A computer generated three dimensional space where users can interact with each other e.g. Second Life is a space where people can converse and even trade online through use of characters representing their online personality.

W

Widget

Web content which can take the form of applications, tools or advertising banners. Web audiences can use widgets to enhance their online experience by customising their digital environment and making it truly personal.

WiFi

(also Wireless local area network) A system that can be used by computers, laptops, PDAs or games consoles in the near vicinity to access the internet.

Wi-Fi can also be used for devices to be connected directly to each other, a function which has been utilised by those playing online or interactive games. An area where a Wi-Fi signal can be received is known as a hot-spot.

Wiki   A collection of websites that allows content to be created, updated or commented on. E.g. Wikipedia or wikispaces.com. Wikis are often used to create collaborative websites or share knowledge across a group of people.

Notes

Notes

Personal Reputation Management Making the internet work for you

Notes

Notes